Table of Contents

Introduction to Docker

Dockers is a command line program, a background daemon, and a suite of remote services that take a logistical approach to solve common software problems and simplify your installation, execution, publishing, and removal software. To do this, use a UNIX technology called containers.

Historically, UNIX-based operating systems have used the term prison to describe a modified execution time of a program that prevents that program from accessing protected sources. Since 2005, after the launch of the Sun Solaris 10 and Solaris 10 tanks, the tank has become the preferred term for such runtime. The goal, which was only to prevent access to protected resources, was to isolate the process from all resources unless explicitly authorized. The use of containers has been a recommended practice for a long time. But the manual construction of a container can be difficult and just plain wrong. This challenge put them out of reach of some, and misconfigured containers inspired others to have a false sense of security. We need a solution to this problem, and Docker helps. Any software that works with Docker runs in the container. Docker uses existing tank motors to ensure consistent tanks are built in accordance with best practices. This puts greater certainty in the reach of everyone. With Docker, customers get low-cost containers. As Docker and his tanks improve, you get the best and latest jailbreak features. Instead of following the fast-paced and highly technical world of building powerful prison prisons, you can let Docker do it for you. This will save you time, money and give you peace of mind.

Containers are not virtualization

Without Docker, organizations often use hardware virtualization (also known as virtual machines) to provide isolation. Virtual machines provide virtual hardware into which the operating system and other programs can be installed. It takes a lot of time (often minutes) to create and require a significant overload of resources as they run a full copy of the operating system except the software you want to use. Unlike virtual machines, Docker containers do not use hardware virtualization. Programs running in Docker containers communicate directly with the Linux host kernel. As there is no additional layer between the program running inside the container and the computer's operating system, resources are not wasted by using redundant software or simulating virtual hardware. This distinction is important. Docker is not virtualization technology. Instead, it helps you use container technology that is already integrated into your operating system.

Running software in insulation tanks

As mentioned earlier, containers have been around for decades. Docker has used namespaces and Linux control groups, which have been part of Linux since 2007. Docker does not offer container technology but makes it easier to use. To understand what containers look like in your system, first establish a baseline. The following illustration shows a basic example that works in a simplified computer system architecture. Note that the command line interface or CLI works in so-called user space memory, as well as other programs running on the operating system. Ideally, programs running in user space cannot alter the memory space of the kernel. In general, the operating system is the interface between all utility programs and the hardware on which the computer runs.

The first is the Docker demon. If installed correctly, this process must always be started. The other is Docker CLI. This is a Docker program that users interact with. If you want to start, stop, or install the software, you will issue a command using Docker. The image below also shows three containers. Each is executed as a secondary process by the Docker daemon, surrounded by a container, and the delegation process is performed in its own user space. Applications running in a container can only access their own memory and resources, as defined by the containers. The containers built by Docker are isolated in eight respects. This section covers each of these aspects through exploring the functionality of the Docker container. The specific aspects are as follows:

• PID namespace: process and feature identifiers

• UTS namespace: host and domain name.

• MNT namespace: access to the file system and structure

• IPC namespace: processing communication in shared memory

• NET site space: network access and structure

• USR namespace: usernames and identifiers

• chroot (): controls the root location of the file system

• Groups: resource protection

Linux namespaces and management groups support runtime containers. Docker uses another set of technologies to secure containers for files that act as shipping containers.

Shipping containers

You can think of a Docker container as a physical shipping container. This is the box where you store and run the application and all its dependencies. Just as cranes, trucks, trains and ships can easily handle shipping containers, so Docker can also easily manage copy and deliver containers. Docker complements the traditional container metaphor by including ways to package and distribute software. The component that serves as the shipping container is called an image. A Docker image is a pooled snapshot of all the files that should be available to a program running in the container. You can create as many image containers as you want. But when they do, the containers running from the same image do not share the changes in their file system. When you distribute software with Docker, you distribute those images to target computers, creating containers. Images are units that can be sent in the Docker ecosystem. Docker provides a set of infrastructure components that simplify Docker image distribution. These components are records and indexes. You may use publicly available infrastructure provided by Docker Inc., other hosting companies, or your records and indexes.

What problems does Docker solve?

• The use of the software is complex. Before installation, you must determine the operating system you are using, the resources required by the software, other installed software, and other software that depends on it. You have to decide where to install it. Then you'll need to know how to install it. Unsurprisingly, installation procedures vary considerably today. The list of considerations is long and ruthless. Software installation is inconsistent and complicated at best. Most computers have several applications installed and running. And most applications depend on other software. What happens when two or more apps you want to use don't work well together? Disaster. Things only get complicated if two or more applications share dependencies:

• What happens if one application requires an updated dependency and the other does not?

• What happens when you delete an application? Is it gone?

• Can old addictions be removed?

• Can you remember the changes you had to make to install the software you want to remove now?

The truth is, the more software you use, the harder it will be to manage it. Even if you can devote the time and energy it takes to install and run applications, how much can you trust for your safety? Open-source and closed-source programs are constantly releasing security updates and it is often impossible to be aware of any issues. The more software you run, the more likely you are to be attacked.

All these problems can be solved with careful accounting, resource management and logistics, but these are everyday and annoying things. Your time would be better spent using the software you are trying to install, update or publish. The people who built Docker have recognized this, and thanks to their hard work, you can easily find a solution as soon as possible. Most of these problems may seem acceptable today. They may feel trivial because you are used to it. After reading how Docker makes these issues accessible, you can find a change in your opinion.

What is Docker for?

Some key practical questions arise: why would you use Docker and for what? The short answer to the "why" is that, with minimal effort, Docker can quickly save your business.

VIRTUAL MACHINE REPLACEMENT (VMS)

Docker can be used to replace virtual machines in many situations. If you're only interested in the application, not the operating system, Docker can replace the virtual machine and let the operating system take care of someone else. Not only does it boot faster than a virtual machine, but it moves more easily, and thanks to a layered file system, you can share changes easier and faster. It is firmly rooted in the command line and is highly programmable.

PROTECTION SOFTWARE

If you want to experiment quickly with the software without disrupting your existing configuration or going through the tedious task of providing a virtual machine, Docker can provide you with an environment much like a sandbox in milliseconds. It is difficult to understand the liberating effect before experiencing it yourself.

PACKAGING SOFTWARE

Since the Docker image doesn't really depend on Linux users, it's a great way to package the software. You can build your own image and ensure that it can run on any modern Linux computer; Think Java, without the need for a JVM.

MICROSERVIC ARCHITECTURE ACTIVATION

Docker makes it easy to decompose a complex system into a number of constituent elements, allowing you to discuss your services more discreetly. This can allow you to restructure your software so that its components are easier to manage and connect without affecting the whole.

NETWORK MODELING

Since you can create hundreds (if not thousands) of isolated containers on one machine, modeling the network is very easy. This can be useful for testing actual scenarios without breaking the bank.

IMPROVES PRODUCTIVITY IN A FULL BATTERY WHEN OUT OF CONNECTION

Because you can group all parts of your system into Docker containers, you can orchestrate them to work on your laptop and work on the go, even offline.

Reduce cleaning costs

The complex negotiation of different teams over the software delivered is a common place in the sector. We have personally experienced countless discussions about damaged libraries. Problematic addictions; updates were applied incorrectly or in the wrong order or were not made at all; non-reproducible insects; et cetera You probably have one too. Docker allows you to clearly indicate (even as a script) the steps you need to follow to solve a problem in a system with known properties, which greatly simplifies the reproduction of errors and environments, which are normally separate from the system. Secured host environment.

Reduce cleaning costs

The complex negotiation of different teams over the software delivered is a common place in the sector. We have personally experienced countless discussions about damaged libraries. problematic addictions; updates were applied incorrectly or in the wrong order or were not made at all; non-reproducible insects; et cetera You probably have one too. Docker allows you to clearly indicate (even as a script) the steps you need to follow to solve a problem in a system with known properties, which greatly simplifies the reproduction of errors and environments, which are normally separate from the system. Secured host environment.

Documentation of software labels and contact points

When you design your images in a structured and ready way for transfer to different environments, Docker asks you to document dependencies on your software explicitly. Even if you to not use Docker everywhere, this documentation can help you install the software elsewhere.

Continuous Delivery (CD) is a paradigm for delivering pipeline based software that with every change reconstructs the system and then goes into production (or "live") through an automated (or partially automated) process. Because it can more accurately control the state of the compilation environment, Docker's constructions are more reproducible and more reversible than traditional software compilation methods. This greatly facilitates the implementation of the CD. Standard CD techniques, such as blue/green implementations (where "real" and "latest" implementations are still active) and Phoenix implementations (where complete systems are updated in each version), are trivial with the application of the game version focused on Docker. process.

Organise

Without Docker, your computer may look like an unwanted tray. Apps have all kinds of dependencies. Some applications rely on system-specific libraries for common tasks such as sound, network, graphics, etc. Others may depend on standard libraries for the language in which they are written. Some others depend on other applications, such as how a Java application depends on a Java virtual machine or a web application may depend on a database. Typically, running a program requires exclusive access to scarce resources, such as a network connection or file. Today, Docker-free applications extend to the entire file system and create a complex network of interactions. Docker keeps things organised by isolating everything with pots and paintings.

Improve portability

Another software issue is that application dependencies typically involve a particular OS. Portability between OSs is a major issue for software users. Although Linux and Mac OS X software compatibility is possible, using the same software on Windows can be more difficult. This may require the creation of full versions of the software. Even this is only possible if there are alternative dependencies that are suitable for Windows. This is a huge effort for application administrators and is often overlooked. Unfortunately for users, a lot of powerful software is difficult, if not impossible to use on your system.

Currently, Docker runs Linux natively and comes with a single virtual machine for OS X and Windows environments. This convergence in Linux means that software running in Docker containers only needs to be written once in a consistent dependency set. You may have thought to yourself, "Wait a minute. You just told me Docker is better than virtual machines." It is true, but these are complementary technologies. Using a virtual machine to contain a unique program is a waste of time. This is especially true of running multiple virtual machines on the same computer. In OS X and Windows, Docker uses one small virtual machine to run all the containers. By adopting this approach, the overhead of running a virtual machine is corrected, while the number of containers can be expanded.

This new portability helps users in many ways. First, open up a world of previously inaccessible software. Second, it is now possible to run the same software, exactly the same software, on any system. This means that the desktop, development environment, business server, and business cloud can run the same programs. Running in harmony with the environment is important. This minimizes any learning curve associated with the adoption of new technologies. This helps software developers better understand the systems that will run their programs. So fewer surprises. Third, when software developers can focus on writing their programs for a single platform and a set of dependencies, this saves them a lot of time and a lot of money for their customers.

Without Dockers or virtual machines, portability is usually achieved at the individual program level by making the software based on a common tool. For example, Java allows developers to write one program that will primarily work on multiple operating systems because they depend on a program called the Java Virtual Machine (JVM). While this is a convenient approach to writing software, other people, other companies have written most of the software we use every day. For example, if there is a popular web server we may want to use but it is not written in Java or any other similar portable language, I suspect that the authors have taken the time to re-write it. With this drawback, language interpreters and software libraries are exactly what creates addiction problems. Docker enhances the portability of each program, regardless of the language in which it was written, the operating system for which it was designed, or the state of the environment in which it is run.

Protect your computer

Most of what I have mentioned so far concerns software usage issues and the benefits of doing things outside the tank. But tanks also protect us from software running inside the container. The program may behave badly or pose a security risk in various ways:

• The program may have been written specifically by the attacker.

• Well-meaning developers could write a program that contains harmful errors.

• The program might inadvertently cause an attacker to handle errors while processing maps.

Running the software compromises the security of your computer. Since the use of software is the most important purpose of a computer, it is wise to apply practical risk mitigation measures. Like physical prison cells, any object contained in a container can access only those contents. There are exceptions to this policy, but only when explicitly created by the user. Containers limit the impact that a program can have on other running programs, data it can access, and system resources. Figure 1.5 shows the difference between running software outside and inside the container. This means for you or your business that the scope of any security threat associated with executing a specific request is limited to the scope of the application itself. Creating powerful application containers is a complex and essential part of any defense strategy in depth. Too often it is ignored or timidly pursued.

Why is Docker important?

Docker provides what is called abstraction. Abstractions let you handle complicated things in a simplified way. So in the case of Docker, instead of focusing on all the complexities and specifics associated with installing an application, we only need to consider the software we want to install. Like a crane that loads a container ship, installing any software with Docker is the same as installing any other software. The shape or size of things inside the shipment may be different, but the way the crane grips the tank will always be the same. All tools can be reused for any container. This goes for eliminating the request as well. When you want to remove the software, simply tell Docker what software to remove. There will be no permanent artifacts as they are all carefully contained and counted. The computer will be as clean as it was before the software was installed.

The abstraction of tanks and tools provided by Docker for working with containers will change the landscape of system administration and software development. Docker is important because it makes containers accessible to everyone. Its use saves time, money and energy.

Another reason why Docker is important is that the software community has a strong incentive to accept container and Docker. The attempt is so strong that companies like Amazon, Microsoft and Google have collaborated to contribute to its development and adopt it in their own cloud offerings. These companies, which mostly disagree, have partnered to support an open source project instead of developing and publishing their own solutions.

The third reason why Docker is important is because it did for the computer what the app stores did for mobile devices. Installing, sharing and removing software are very easy. Better yet, Docker does this openly and across multiple platforms. Imagine all the major smartphones sharing the same app store. That would be a big problem. With this technology implemented, it is possible that the lines between operating systems will finally begin to fade and that third-party vendor offerings play a less important role in operating system selection.

Fourth, we are finally starting to better adopt some of the most advanced features of operating system isolation. This may seem small, but many people try to further protect their computers by isolating them at the operating system level. Too bad his hard work took so long to be mass-adopted. Containers have been in one way or another for decades. It's great that Docker helps us make the most of these features.

Where and when to use Docker

Docker can be used on most computers at work and at home. In particular, how far does it go? Docker can work almost anywhere, but that doesn't mean you want to do it. For example, Docker can currently only run applications that can run on the Linux operating system. This means that if you want to execute native OS X or Windows, you still can't do it through Docker. For example, by restricting the conversation to software that typically runs on a Linux server or workstation, it is possible to create a solid scenario for running most applications in the container. This includes server applications such as web servers, mail servers, databases, proxy servers, etc. Desktop software like web browsers, word processors, email clients or other tools is also very useful. Even trusted programs are just as dangerous to run as programs you download from the Internet if they interact with user-provided data or online data.

Running in the tank and as a user with reduced privileges will help protect your system from attack. In addition to the added benefits of defense, using Docker for everyday tasks helps keep your computer clean. Keeping your computer clean will help prevent common resource issues and make it easier to install and remove software. This same ease of installation, removal and distribution simplifies IT management and can drastically change the way organizations think about maintenance. The most important thing to remember is when the containers are inappropriate.

The tanks will not help much for the safety of the programs that have to work with full access to the machine. At the time of writing, this is possible but complicated. Containers are not a complete solution to security issues, but they can also be used to prevent many types of attacks. Remember, you must not use software from unreliable sources. This is especially true if this software requires administrator privileges. This means that it is a bad idea to blindly manage the containers delivered by the customer in a jointly implanted environment.

Installation / Installation Programs

Installers are, of course, one of the first pieces you need to use Docker on your local computer as well as in server environments.

First, in what environments can you install Docker:

• Linux (various types of Linux)

• Apple macOS

• Windows 10 Professional

In addition, you can launch them in public clouds such as Amazon Web Services, Microsoft Azure and DigitalOcean. With the different types of installers listed, Docker operates in different ways in the operating system. Docker runs natively on Linux; therefore, if you are using Linux, the way Docker runs directly on your system is very simple. However, if you're using MacOS or Windows 10, it works a little differently because it is Linux based.

Linux Installation (Ubuntu 16.04)

As mentioned earlier, this is the simplest installation of the three systems we will test. To install Docker, simply run the following command from a Terminal session:

```
$ curl -sSL https://get.docker.com/ | sh
$ sudosystemctl docker
```

These commands will download, install, and configure the latest version of Docker from Docker. At the time of writing the version of the Linux operating system installed with the official software

The installation script is 5/17/05.

Running the following command should confirm that Docker is installed and running:

```
$ docker version
```

MacOS installation

Unlike the Linux command line installation, Docker for Mac has a graphical installer.

Before downloading, be sure to use ApplemacOS Yosemite 10.10.3 or later. If you use an older version, there is no lost; You can still run Docker.

You can download the Docker Store installer at http://store.docker.com/editions/community/docker-this- desktop-mac

Just click on Get Docker. After downloading, you will get a DMG file. Mount the image, and opening a desktop-mounted image should show you something like this:

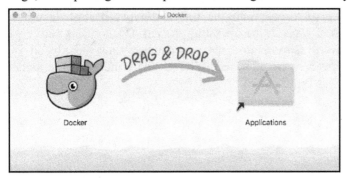

When you have hauled the Docker icon to your Applications folder, double tap on it and you will be asked whether you need to open the application you have downloaded. Saying yes will open the Docker installer:

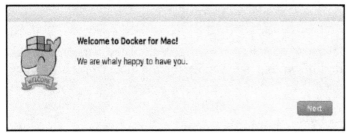

Click Next and follow the on-screen instructions. Once installed and running, you should see the Docker icon in the icon bar in the upper left corner of the screen.

Installation in Windows 10 Professional

Like Docker for Mac, Docker for Windows uses a graphical installer. Before downloading, be sure to use Microsoft Windows 10 Professional or 64-bit Enterprise. If you are running an older version or unsupported edition of Windows 10, you can still run Docker. See Other legacy operating systems in this chapter for more information.

Docker for Windows has this requirement due to Hyper-V dependency. Hyper-V is a native Windows hypervisor and allows you to run x86-64 guests on your Windows PC, either Windows 10 Professional or Windows Server. It's even part of the XBox One operating system.

You can download Docker for Windows from the Docker Store at https://store.docker.com/editions/community/docker-th- desktop-windows /; Simply click the Docker button to download the installer. After downloading, start the MSI package.

Click Install, and then follow the instructions, which will not only work during Docker installation but will enable Hyper-V if you did not enable it. After installation, you should see the Docker icon in the icon bar in the lower right corner of the screen.

Run the software in containers

In this chapter, you will understand all the basics of container operations and how Docker helps resolve clutter and conflict issues. You will review examples of Docker features as you can find them daily.

See the Docker command line for help

Use the Docker command line utility in the rest of this book. To start, I want to show you how to get information about the commands of the program itself with fixed menus. This will help you understand how to use the correct version of Docker on your computer. Open a terminal or command prompt and execute the following command:

the help of docker

Running Docker Help shows basic syntax information for using the Docker command line program, as well as a complete list of commands for your version of the program. Try it and take a moment to admire all the interesting things you can do.

Docker's help only gives you high-level information about the available commands. To get detailed info about a command, include the command in the <COMMAND> argument. For example, you can enter the following command to learn how to copy files from a location inside a container to a location on the host computer:

help docker cp

The usage pattern for dockercp will be shown, a general description of what the command should do, and a detailed overview of its arguments. I'm sure you will have a great time executing the order in the rest of this book, now that you know how to seek help if you need it.

Container control: Creating a monitor for a site

Most of the examples in this book will use real software. Practical examples will help you introduce Docker features and illustrate how you will use them in your daily activities. In this first example, you will install a web server called NGINX. Web servers are programs that make the files and programs of the site available to web browsers through the network. Do not create a site, but you will install and run a web server using Docker. If you follow these instructions, the web server will only be available for other programs on your computer.

Suppose a new customer enters your office and makes a scandalous offer to create a new website. They want a strictly monitored website. This individual customer wants to perform their own operations. Therefore, you want the solution you provide to be emailed to your computer when the server is down. They have also heard about this popular web server software called NGINX and have specifically asked you to use it. After learning about the benefits of working with Docker, he decided to use it for this project.

Create and run a new container

When we install software with Docker, we say we install the image. There are several methods to install an image and several sources. In this example, we will download and install an image for NGINX from Docker Hub. Please note that the Docker Hub is a public recording provided by Docker Inc. The NGINX image comes from what Docker Inc. calls the approved repository.

Usually, the person or foundation that publishes the software controls the secure repositories for that software. Executing the following command will download, install, and run a container running NGINX:

Docker Run - Add \
--name web nginx: last

After you run this command, Docker will install nginx: last from the NGINX repository located on the Docker Hub and run the software. After Docker installed and started NGINX, a line of apparently random characters is written to the terminal. It will look like this:

7cb5d2b9a7eab87f07182b5bf58936c9947890995b1b94f412912fa822a9ecb5

This character line is a unique container identifier just created to run NGINX. Whenever you run Docker and create a new container, this container will receive a similar unique identifier. It is common for users to capture this output with a variable they use with other commands. You don't need do this for this example. Once the ID is displayed, it may appear that nothing has happened. This is because he used the --detach option and started the program in the background. This means that the application has started but is not connected to your device. It makes sense to run NGINX this way because we will run some different programs.

Running separate containers is ideal for background programs. This type of program is called a daemon. A demon usually communicates with other programs or people through a network or other communication tool. When launching a daemon or other program in the container that you want to run in the background, be sure to use the --detach flag or its abbreviated form, -d.

Another demon your client needs is advertising. The sender is waiting for the caller's connection and sending the email. The following command will install and run an email application that will work for this example:

docker run -d \
--name mailer \

This command uses the truncated flag form --detach to run a new mailbox called mailer in the background. At this point, he made two orders and provided two-thirds of the systems his client wanted. The last component, called the agent, is perfect for the interactive container.

Executing interactive containers

Programs that can interact with users tend to feel more interactive. A good example is a text editor on a terminal. The Docker command line tool is a perfect example of an interactive terminal program. These types of programs can receive input from users or show output at a terminal. To run interactive programs in Docker, you need to connect parts of your device to the input or output of the bootable container. To get started using interactive containers, run the following command:

Docker Run - interactive - tty \
- internet connection: web \
- Web_test name \
busy: last / bin / sh

The command uses two flags in the execution command: - interactive (or -i) and - ttty (or -t). First, the --interactive option tells Docker to keep the standard input sequence (stdin) open for the container, even if the terminal is not connected. Second, the --tyty option tells Docker to assign a virtual terminal to the container, which will allow it to send a signal to the container. This is usually what you look for in an interactive command line program. You will usually use them when you run the interactive program as a shell in an interactive container.

As important as the interactive metrics are, when you started this container, you specified the program to run inside the container. In this case, he ran a shell program called sh. You can run any available program in the container. The interactive container sample command creates a container, starts a UNIX shell, and is associated with a container that runs NGINX. From this shell, you can execute the command to check that your web server is working properly:

wget -O- http: // web: 80 /

This uses a program called wget to send an HTTP request to a web server (a NGINX server that was previously run in the container) and then display the contents of the web page on your device. There may be a message like "Welcome to NGINX!" at this point.

Everything is working properly and you can continue and stop this interactive container by typing the output. This will interrupt the shell program and stop the tank. You can create an interactive container, manually start the process inside that container, and then disconnect the device. You can do that holding the Crtl (or Control) key and pressing P, then Q. This will only work if you used the --tty option. To complete a client job, you need to run an agent. What does this mean?

This is an agent that will test the web server as in the previous example and send a message to the sender if the web server stops. This command is triggered by an agent in an interactive container using abbreviated indicators:

docker run -it \
- agent's name \
- web link: insideweb \
- Email link: Insidemailer \
dockerinaction / ch2_agent

When done, the mailbox will test the web mailbox every second and print a message like this:

System in place.

Now that you know what you are doing, detach the terminal from the tank. Specifically, when you start the tank and start typing "System On," press and hold the Ctrl (or Control) key, then press P, then Q. Then you will return to the shell of your computer. the host. Don't stop the program; otherwise, the monitor will stop checking the web server. Although you usually use separate containers or daemons for software you deploy to network servers, interactive containers are very useful for running software on your desktop or for manual work on a server. At this point, you have launched all three applications in the mailboxes that your client needs. Before you can rightly pretend to complete, you need to test the system.

List, shut down, restart, and view the production of the container.

The first thing you need to test your current configuration is to check which containers are running with the dockerps command:

dockerps

Executing the command will show the following information about each container being executed:

• container identifier
• the image used
• command executed in container
• the time elapsed since the tank was created
• the duration of the tank
• Network ports exposed by tank.
• container name

At this point, you must have three mailboxes named: Web, Email, and Agent. If one is missing but you have followed the example so far, it may have stopped by mistake. This is not a problem as Docker has a command to restart the container. The following three commands restart each container using the container name. Select the appropriate ones to restart the missing containers in the mailbox list.

restart the web
docker resets mail

Restart Agent

Now that all the containers are running, you should check that the system is working properly. The best way to do so is to review the records of each container. Get started with the web container:

Docker blogs

This should show long records with several lines containing this subpage:

"GET / HTTP / 1.0" 200

The web server is up and running and the agent is testing the site. Each time an agent tests a site, one of these lines is entered in the registry. The dockerlogs command may be useful in these cases, but it is dangerous to believe in it. Anything written by the program in the output string stdout or stderr will be recorded in this register. The problem with this model is that the record is never rotated or truncated, so the data written in the container record remains and expands as long as the container contains indexes. This long-term persistence can be a problem for long-term processes.

You may know that the agent controls the web server by examining only the web logs. To complete, you must examine the registry and mail agent exit log:

Docker commercial
Docker Registration Agent

Mail-order newspapers should look like this:

The CH2 Mailer example is running.

Agent records must contain several lines, such as the one you looked at when you started the container:

System in place.

Now that you have verified that the mailboxes are running and that the agent is able to reach the web server, you should check that the web server notices that the web container has stopped. When this happens, the agent must activate the call to the sender and the event must be recorded in the agent and sender records. The stop docker command tells the program with PID # 1 in the container to stop. Use it in the following system test commands:

docker stop web
Docker commercial

Look for the line at the end of the mail record that says the following:

"Send an email to admin @ work Message: service shut down!"

This line indicates that the agent has successfully detected the NGINX server interrupt on the named web site. Congratulations. Your client will be happy and will build their first real container and Docker system.

Learning the basic features of Docker is one thing, but understanding the reasons to use them and build them for more complete systems is another. The best place to start learning is the namespace of the process identifier provided by Linux.

Fixed issues and PID namespace

Each program or process running on a Linux computer has a unique number called the Process Identifier (PID). A PID namespace is a set of possible numbers that identifies processes. Linux provides the ability to create multiple PID namespaces. Each namespace has a full set of available PIDs. That means that each PID namespace will contain its own PID, like 1, 2, 3, etc. From a process standpoint in one namespace, the PID 1 startup process can be called runit or supervisor. In another namespace, PID 1 may call the shell command bash. Creating a PID with namespaces for each container is a key feature of Docker. Do the following to see it in action:

```
docker run -d - namespaceA \ busybox: last / bin / sh -c "sleep 30000"
docker run -d - nameBB \

occupied: last / bin / sh -c "nc -l -p 0.0.0.0:80"
```

docker exec namespaceA ps docker exec namespaceB ps

The command above should generate a list of processes similar to this:

PID USER COMMAND
1 root / bucket / sh -c sleep 30000
5 roots of sleep 30000
6 roots ps

The command above should generate a slightly different list of processes:

PID USER COMMAND
1 root / bin / sh -c nc -l -p 0.0.0.0:80
7 root nc -l -p 0.0.0.0:80
8 ps root

In this example, use the dock exec command to perform additional processes in the current container. In this case, the command you are using is called ps. Displays all current processes and their PIDs. On departure, it is clear that each container has a PID 1 process.

Without the PID namespace, processes running in the container would share the same identifier as those in other containers or the host. The container can determine what other processes took place on the main machine. Even worse, namespaces turn many licensing decisions into domain decisions. This means that processes in one container can control the processes of other containers. A docker would be much less useful without the PID namespace. Linux features used by Docker, such as namespaces, help you solve all kinds of software issues.

Like most Docker features, you can optionally create containers without your own PID space. You can test it yourself by configuring the --pid flag to create a Docker or run the Docker and set the value as the host. Try it yourself with the container running BusyBox Linux and the ps Linux command:
Docker - Busy Host Host: Last ps

Take the previous example of network monitoring. Let's say you don't use Docker and simply run NGINX directly on your computer. Let's say you forgot that you already started NGINX for another project. When you restart NGINX, the second process will not be able to access the required resources because the first process already has them. This is an example of a basic software conflict. You can see it in action when trying to run two copies of NGINX in the same container:

docker run - d - name webConflict nginx: last

docker registers webConflict

```
docker executive webConflict nginx - g 'daemon off;'
```

The last command should display the output as follows:

03/29/2015. 04/22/35 [emerg] 10 # 0: connection () to 0.0.0.0:80 failed (98:

Address already used

nginx: [popup] bind () in 0.0.0.0:80 failed (98: address already used)

The subsequent methodology doesn't begin accurately and demonstrates that the necessary location is as of now being utilized. This is called port clash and is a typical issue in genuine frameworks where numerous procedures run on a similar PC or a few people add to a similar situation. This is an incredible case of a contention of issues that Docker rearranges and explains. Run every one out of an alternate compartment, for example, this one:

To make speculations regarding potential clashes between programs, think about the illustration of stopping. Paid stopping has some fundamental highlights: an installment framework, some saved parking spots, and numbered spaces.

By associating these capacities to a PC framework, the installment framework is a mutual asset with a particular interface. The installment framework can acknowledge money or Mastercards, or both. Individuals who convey just cash won't have the option to utilize the carport with an installment framework that acknowledges just Mastercards, and individuals without cash who pay charges won't have the option to stop in the carport.

Likewise, programs that rely upon a typical segment, for example, a specific form of a programming language library, can't run on PCs with another rendition of this library or without this library. Like two individuals utilizing if another installment technique needs to be stopped in a similar carport that acknowledges just a single strategy, a contention happens when you need to utilize two programs that require various forms of the library.

The held spaces in this similitude speak to uncommon assets. Envision a leaving chaperon apportioning a similar space for two autos. Albeit just a single driver needs to utilize the carport at once, no issue. Be that as it may, if both need to utilize the space simultaneously, the previous successes and the last can't stop. As you will see from the case of contention in Section 2.7, this is a similar kind of contention as when two projects endeavor to associate with a similar system port.

Ultimately, consider what might occur on the off chance that somebody changed their leaving numbers while the vehicles were left. At the point when proprietors return and attempt to find their vehicles, they will most likely be unable to do as such. While this is a strange model, it is an incredible representation to recognise what occurs in programs when basic natural factors change. Projects frequently use condition factors or library sections to discover different assets they need. These assets might be libraries or various projects. At the point when projects conflict, these factors may change conflictingly.

Here are some normal issues with strife:

■ Two projects need to interface with a similar system port.

■ Two projects utilize a similar impermanent document name, which keeps the record from being bolted.

■ Two projects need to utilise various renditions of the all around introduced library.

■ Two duplicates of a similar program need to utilise the same PID record.

■ Another program you introduced changed nature variable utilised by the other program. Presently the primary program has been ended.

These contentions happen when at least one projects share a typical reliance; however, can't acknowledge sharing or have various needs. As in the past port clash model, Docker settles programming clashes with apparatuses, for example, Linux namespaces, the foundation of the document framework, and virtualised arrange segments. These devices are utilised to disengage every compartment.

Container state and dependencies

Eliminating metaconflicts: building a website farm

In the last area, you perceived how Docker causes you to maintain a strategic distance from programming clashes with process disengagement. Be that as it may, in case you're not cautious, you can wind up building frameworks that make metaconflicts, or clashes between compartments in the Docker layer.

Consider another model where a customer has requested that you manufacture a framework where you can have a variable number of sites for their clients. They'd likewise prefer to utilize a similar observing innovation that you manufactured before in this section. Basically growing the framework you constructed before would be the most straightforward approach to complete this activity without redoing the design for NGINX. In this model, you'll fabricate a sys-tem with a few holders running web servers and an observing operator (specialist) for each web server.

One's first intuition may be to just begin more web holders. That is not as sim-ple as it sounds. Recognizing compartments gets confused as the quantity of holders increments.

Adaptable holder distinguishing proof

The most ideal approach to discover why essentially making more duplicates of the NGINX holder you utilized in the last model is a poorly conceived notion is to attempt it for yourself:

```
docker run   -d    - - name    webid nginx
docker run   -d    - - name    webid nginx
```

The second order here will fall flat with a contention mistake:

FATA[0000] Error reaction from daemon: Conflict. The name "webid" is as of now being used by holder 2b5958ba6a00. You need to erase (or rename) that holder to have the option to reuse that name.

Utilizing fixed holder names like the web is helpful for experimentation and documenta-tion, however in a framework with different compartments, utilizing fixed names like that can make clashes. Of course, Docker appoints a one of a kind (human-accommodating) name to each con-tainer it makes. The - name banner essentially abrogates that procedure with a known worth. If a situation rises where the name of a holder needs to change, you can, by and large, rename the compartment with the docker rename course:

docker rename webid webid-old

docker run - d - - name webid nginx

Renaming compartments can help ease one-off naming clashes yet does little to help keep away from the issue in any case. Notwithstanding the name, Docker doles out an interesting identifier that was referenced in the primary model. These are hex-encoded 1024-piece numbers and look something like this:

7cb5d2b9a7eab87f07182b5bf58936c9947890995b1b94f412912fa822a9ecb5

At the point when compartments are begun in isolates mode, their identifier will be printed to the terminal. You can utilize these identifiers instead of the compartment name with any com-mand that necessities to distinguish a particular holder. For instance, you could utilize the previ-ous ID with a stop or executive order:

docker executive \

7cb5d2b9a7eab87f07182b5bf58936c9947890995b1b94f412912fa822a9ecb5 \

ps

docker stop \

7cb5d2b9a7eab87f07182b5bf58936c9947890995b1b94f412912fa822a9ecb5

The high likelihood of uniqueness of the IDs that are produced implies that it is improbable that there will ever be an impact with this ID. To a lesser degree, it is additionally impossible that there would even be a crash of the initial 12 characters of this ID on a similar PC. So in most Docker interfaces, you'll see holder IDs truncated to their initial 12 characters. This makes produced IDs more easy to use. You can utilize them any place a compartment identifier is required. So the past two directions could be composed this way:

docker executive 7cb5d2b9a7ea ps

docker stop 7cb5d2b9a7ea

Neither of these IDs is especially appropriate for human use. In any case, they work very well with contents and computerisation systems. Docker has a few methods for getting the ID of a compartment to make computerisation conceivable. In these cases, the full or truncated numeric ID will be utilized.
The primary method to get the numeric ID of a compartment is to begin or make another one and relegate the aftereffect of the order to a shell variable. As you saw before, when another compartment is begun in disconnected mode, the holder ID

will be kept in touch with the terminal (stdout). You'd be not able to utilize this with intelligent holders if this were the best way to get the compartment ID at creation time. Fortunately, you can utilize another direction to make a holder without beginning it. The docker makes direction is fundamentally the same as docker run; the essential distinction is that the holder is made in a halted state:

docker make nginx

The outcome ought to be a line like:

b26a631e536d3caae348e9fd36e7661254a11511eb2274fb55f9f7c788721b0d

In case you're utilizing a Linux order shell like sh or slam, you can essentially appoint that outcome to a shell variable and use it again later:

CID=$(docker make nginx: latest)

reverberation $CID

Shell factors make another open door for strife, yet the extent of that contention is constrained to the terminal session or current handling condition that the content was propelled in. Those contentions ought to be effectively avoidable in light of the fact that one utilize or program is dealing with that condition. The issue with this methodology is that it won't help if various clients or robotized forms need to share that data. In those cases you can utilize a holder ID (CID) document.

Both the docker run and docker make directions give another banner to compose the ID of another holder to a known document:

docker make - cidfile/tmp/web.cid nginx

Like the utilization of shell factors, this element builds the open door for struggle. The name of the CID record (gave after - cidfile) must be known or have some known structure. Much the same as manual holder naming, this methodology utilizes known names in a worldwide (Docker-wide) namespace. Fortunately Docker won't make another holder utilizing the gave CID record if that document as of now exists. The direction will bomb similarly as it does when you make two holders with a similar name.

One motivation to utilize CID documents rather than names is that CID records can be imparted to holders effectively and renamed for that compartment. This uses a Docker include called volumes, which is shrouded in part 4.

TIP One technique for managing CID document naming crashes is to parcel the namespace by utilizing known or unsurprising way shows. For instance, in this situation, you may utilize a way that contains all web compartments under a known index and further segment that registry by the client ID. This would bring about a way like/holders/web/customer1/web.cid or/contain-ers/web/customer8/web.cid.

In various cases, you can use various headings like docker ps to get the ID of a container. For example, if you have to get the truncated ID of the last made holder, you can use this:
CID=$(docker ps - most recent - calm)

reverberation $CID

CID=$(docker ps - l – q)

reverberation $CID

TIP If you need to get the full holder ID, you can utilize the - no-trunc choice on the docker ps direction.

Robotization cases are secured by the highlights you've seen up until this point. In any case, despite the fact that truncation helps, these holder IDs are once in a while simple to peruse or recollect. For this rea-child, Docker additionally produces comprehensible names for every holder.

The naming show utilizes an individual descriptor, an underscore, and the last name of a compelling researcher, architect, creator, or another such idea pioneer. Instances of produced names are compassionate_swartz, hungry_goodall, and distracted_turing. These appear to hit a sweet spot for meaningfulness and memory. At the point when you're working with the docker apparatus legitimately, you can generally utilize docker ps to look into the human-accommodating names.

Compartment recognizable proof can be precarious, yet you can deal with the issue by utilizing the ID and name-age highlights of Docker.

Container state and dependencies

With this new information, the new framework may looks something like this:

MAILER_CID=$(docker run   -d dockerinaction/ch2_mailer)

WEB_CID=$(docker create   nginx)

AGENT_CID=$(docker make - connect $WEB_CID:insideweb \ - interface $MAILER_CID:insidemailer \ dockerinaction/ch2_agent)

This piece could be utilized to seed another content that dispatches another NGINX and operator example for every one of your customer's clients. You can utilize docker ps to see that they've been made:

docker ps

The explanation neither the NGINX nor the operator was incorporated with the yield has to do with holder state. Docker holders will consistently be in one of four states and transi-tion by means of order

Neither of the new holders you began shows up in the rundown of compartments since docker ps shows just showing holders to default. Those compartments were specifi-cally made with docker make and never began (the left state). To see every one of the holders (counting those in the left state), utilize the - an alternative:

docker ps - a

Since you've checked that both of the holders were made, you have to begin them. For that, you can utilize the docker start direction:

docker start $AGENT_CID

docker start $WEB_CID

Running those directions will bring about a mistake. The holders should be begun the backward request of their reliance chain. Since you attempted to begin the specialist con-tainer before the web compartment, Docker revealed a message like this one:

Mistake reaction from daemon: Cannot begin holder
03e65e3c6ee34e714665a8dc4e33fb19257d11402b151380ed4c0a5e38779d0a: Cannot connection to a non running compartment:/clever_wright AS/modest_hopper/insideweb

FATA[0000] Error: neglected to begin at least one compartments

In this model, the operator holder has a reliance on the web compartment. You have to begin the web compartment first:

docker start $WEB_CID

docker start $AGENT_CID

This bodes well when you think about the mechanics at work. The connection system infuses IP addresses into subordinate compartments, and holders that aren't running don't have IP addresses. On the off chance that you attempted to begin a holder that has a reliance on a compartment that isn't running, Docker wouldn't have an IP address to infuse. Compartment connecting is shrouded in part 5, yet it's valuable to show this significant point in beginning holders.

Regardless of whether you're utilizing docker run or docker make, the subsequent holders should be begun in the turn around the request of their reliance chain. This implies circular conditions are difficult to assemble utilizing Docker compartment connections.

Now you can assemble everything into one succinct content that resembles the accompanying:

MAILER_CID=$(docker run - d dockerinaction/ch2_mailer)

WEB_CID=$(docker run - d nginx)

AGENT_CID=$(docker run - d \

- connect $WEB_CID:insideweb \

- connect $MAILER_CID:insidemailer \

dockerinaction/ch2_agent)

Presently you're sure that this content can be run no matter what each time your client necessities to arrangement another site. Your customer has returned and expressed gratitude toward you for the web and checking work you've finished up until this point, however things have changed.

They've chosen to concentrate on building their sites with WordPress (a prevalent open source content-administration and blogging program). Fortunately, WordPress is bar lished through Docker Hub in a store named wordpress:4. All you'll have to

convey is a lot of directions to arrangement another WordPress site that has a similar checking and cautioning highlights that you've just conveyed.

The intriguing thing about substance the executive's frameworks and other stateful systems is that the information they work with makes each running system particular. Adam's WordPress blog is unique in relation to Betty's WordPress blog, regardless of whether they're running similar programming. Just the substance is extraordinary. Regardless of whether the substance is the equivalent, they're diverse because they're running on various destinations.

On the off chance that you construct frameworks or programming that know a lot about their condition—like locations or fixed areas of reliance benefits—it's hard to change that condition or reuse the product. You have to convey a framework that limits environment reliance before the agreement is finished.

A significant part of the work related to introducing programming or keeping up an armada of PCs lies in managing specializations of the registering condition. These specializations come as worldwide perused conditions (like realized host document framework areas), hard-coded sending structures (condition checks in code or configura-tion), or information region (information put away on a specific PC outside the organization design). Knowing this, if you probably manufacture low-support frameworks, you ought to endeavor to limit these things.

Docker has three definite highlights to help construct condition rationalist frameworks:

- Read-just document frameworks
- Environment variable infusion
- Volumes

Working with volumes is a major subject and the theme of part 4. So as to gain proficiency with the initial two highlights, consider necessities change for the model circumstance utilized in the remainder of this section.

WordPress utilizes a database program called MySQL to store a large portion of its information, so it's a smart thought, to begin with ensuring that a compartment running WordPress has a perused just record framework.
Peruse just document frameworks
Utilizing read-just record frameworks achieves two positive things. In the first place, you can have con-fidence that the holder won't be specific from changes to the documents it contains. Second, you have expanded certainty that an assailant can't bargain records in the holder.

To begin chipping away at your customer's framework, make and start a compartment from the WordPress picture utilizing the - read-just banner:
docker run - d - name wp - read-just wordpress:4
At the point when this is done, watch that the compartment is running. You can do so utilizing any of the strategies presented already, or you can examine the holder metadata

straightforwardly. The accompanying direction will print genuine if the holder named wp is running and bogus generally.

docker review - group "{{.State.Running}}" wp

The docker review order will show all the metadata (a JSON record) that Docker keeps up for a holder. The organization choice changes that metadata, and for this situation, it channels everything with the exception of the field demonstrating the running condition of the holder. This order should yield bogus.

For this situation, the compartment isn't running. To decide why inspect the logs for the holder:
docker logs wp
That should yield something like:

error: missing WORDPRESS_DB_HOST and MYSQL_PORT_3306_TCP condition factors
Did you neglect to - interface some_mysql_container:mysql or set an outer db with - e WORDPRESS_DB_HOST=hostname: port?

WordPress has a reliance on a MySQL database. A database is a star gram that stores information so that it's retrievable and accessible later. Fortunately, you can introduce MySQL utilising Docker simply like WordPress:

docker run - d - name wpdb \

- e MYSQL_ROOT_PASSWORD=ch2demo \

mysql:5
When that is begun, make an alternate WordPress holder that is connected to this new database compartment:

docker run   -d - name wp2 \

- link   wpdb:mysql \

- p   80 - read-just \

wordpress:4

Check once again that WordPress is running effectively:

docker assess - group "{{.State.Running}}" wp2

You can advise that WordPress neglected to begin once more. Inspect the logs to decide the reason:

docker logs wp2

There ought to be a line in the logs that is like the accompanying:

... Peruse just record framework: AH00023: Couldn't make the revamp map mutex (document/var/lock/apache2/revise map.1)

You can advise that WordPress neglected to begin once more, yet this time the issue is that it's attempting to compose a lock record to a particular area. This is a necessary piece of the startup

Make explicit volumes for writeable space

Process and isn't a specialization. It's proper to make a special case to the read-just document framework for this situation. You have to utilize a volume to make that exemption. Utilize the accompanying to begin WordPress with no issues:

```
#       Start the compartment with explicit volumes for read just exemptions docker
run - d - name wp3 - connect wpdb:mysql - p 80 \

- v/run/lock/apache2/\ - v/run/apache2/\ - read-just wordpress:4
```

A refreshed form of the content you've been dealing with should resemble this:

```
SQL_CID=$(docker make - e MYSQL_ROOT_PASSWORD=ch2demo mysql:5)
```

```
docker start $SQL_CID
```

```
MAILER_CID=$(docker make dockerinaction/ch2_mailer)
```

```
docker start $MAILER_CID
```

```
WP_CID=$(docker make - interface $SQL_CID:mysql - p 80 \ - v/run/lock/apache2/ -
v/run/apache2/\ - read-just wordpress:4)
```

```
docker start $WP_CID
```

```
AGENT_CID=$(docker make - connect $WP_CID:insideweb \ - interface
$MAILER_CID:insidemailer \ dockerinaction/ch2_agent)
```

```
docker start $AGENT_CID
```

Congrats, now you ought to have a running WordPress holder! By utilising a read-just document framework and connecting WordPress to another compartment running a database, you can be certain that the holder running the WordPress picture will never show signs of change. This implies if there is consistently some problem with the PC running a customer's WordPress blog, you ought to have the option to fire up another duplicate of that holder somewhere else without any issues.

Be that as it may, there are two issues with this structure. To start with, the database is running in a con-tainer on a similar PC as the WordPress holder. Second, WordPress is utilising a few defaults esteems for significant settings like database name, authoritative client, secret managerial phrase, database salt, etc. To manage this issue, you could make a few adaptations of the WordPress programming, each with an extraordinary setup for the customer. Doing so would transform your straightforward provisioning content into a beast that makes pictures and composes documents. A superior method to infuse that arrangement would be using condition factors.

Condition variable infusion

Condition factors are key-esteem matches that are made accessible to programs through their execution setting. They let you change a program's arrangement without altering any records or changing the direction used to begin the program.

Docker utilizes condition factors to convey data about ward holders, the host name of the compartment, and other helpful data for expert grams running in chambers. Docker likewise gives a component to a client to infuse condition factors into another holder. Projects that know to expect significant data through condition factors can be designed at compartment creation time. Fortunately for you and your customer, WordPress is one such program.

Before jumping into WordPress points of interest, take a stab at infusing and survey condition vari-ables all alone. The UNIX direction env shows all the earth factors in the present execution setting (your terminal). To see condition variable infusion in real life, utilize the accompanying order:

docker run - env MY_ENVIRONMENT_VAR="this is a test" \

busybox:latest \

env

The - env banner—or - e for short—can be utilized to infuse any condition variable. On the off chance that the variable is as of now set by the picture or Docker, at that point the worth will be abrogated. Along these lines, programs running inside holders can depend on the factors continually being set. WordPress watches the accompanying condition factors:

- WORDPRESS_DB_HOST
- WORDPRESS_DB_USER
- WORDPRESS_DB_PASSWORD
- WORDPRESS_DB_NAME
- WORDPRESS_AUTH_KEY
- WORDPRESS_SECURE_AUTH_KEY
- WORDPRESS_LOGGED_IN_KEY
- WORDPRESS_NONCE_KEY
- WORDPRESS_AUTH_SALT
- WORDPRESS_SECURE_AUTH_SALT
- WORDPRESS_LOGGED_IN_SALT
- WORDPRESS_NONCE_SALT

TIP This model dismisses the KEY and SALT factors, yet any genuine creation framework should completely set these qualities.

To begin, you should address the issue that the database is running in a compartment on a similar PC as the WordPress holder. As opposed to utilizing connecting to fulfill WordPress' database reliance, infuse an incentive for the WORDPRESS_DB_HOST variable:

docker make - env WORDPRESS_DB_HOST=<my database hostname> wordpress:4

This model would make (not begin) a compartment for WordPress that will attempt to interface with a MySQL database at whatever you determine at <my database hostname>.

Since the remote database isn't likely utilizing any default client name or secret word, you'll need to infuse esteems for those settings too. Assume the database head is a feline sweetheart and detests solid passwords:

docker make \

- env WORDPRESS_DB_HOST=<my database hostname> \ - env WORDPRESS_DB_USER=site_admin \

- env WORDPRESS_DB_PASSWORD=MeowMix42 \

wordpress:4

Utilizing condition variable infusion along these lines will assist you with isolating the physical ties between a WordPress holder and a MySQL compartment. Indeed, even for the situation where you need to have the database and your client WordPress locales all on a similar machine, regardless you'll have to fix the subsequent issue referenced before. Every one of the destinations are utilizing a similar default database name. You'll have to utilize condition variable infusion to set the database name for every free site:

docker create - connect wpdb:mysql \

- e   WORDPRESS_DB_NAME=client_a_wp wordpress:4   For customer A

docker create - interface wpdb:mysql \   For customer B

- e   WORDPRESS_DB_NAME=client_b_wp wordpress:4

Since you've tackled these issues, you can change the provisioning content. To begin with, set the PC to run just a solitary MySQL compartment:

DB_CID=$(docker run - d - e MYSQL_ROOT_PASSWORD=ch2demo mysql:5)

MAILER_CID=$(docker run - d dockerinaction/ch2_mailer)

At that point the site provisioning content would be this:

on the off chance that [! - n "$CLIENT_ID"]; at that point reverberation "Customer ID not set" leave 1

```
fi

WP_CID=$(docker make \

- interface $DB_CID:mysql \

- name wp_$CLIENT_ID \

- p 80 \

- v/run/lock/apache2/ - v/run/apache2/\

- e WORDPRESS_DB_NAME=$CLIENT_ID \

- read-just wordpress:4)

docker start $WP_CID

AGENT_CID=$(docker make \

- name agent_$CLIENT_ID \

- connect $WP_CID:insideweb \

- connect $MAILER_CID:insidemailer \

dockerinaction/ch2_agent)

docker start $AGENT_CID
```

This new content will begin a case of WordPress and the checking operator for every client and associate those holders to one another just as a single mailer star gram and MySQL database. The WordPress compartments can be wrecked, restarted, and updated with no stress over loss of information.

The customer ought to be satisfied with what is being conveyed. However, one thing may be annoying you. In prior testing, you found that the checking operator accurately advised the mailer when the site was inaccessible, however restarting the site and specialist required manual work. It would be better if the framework attempted to recuperate when a disappointment was identified consequently. Docker furnishes restart strategies to help manage that, yet you may need something increasingly vigorous.

Building strong holders

There are situations where programming bombs in uncommon conditions that are brief in nature. Despite the fact that it's imperative to be made mindful when these conditions emerge, it's for the most part in any event as critical to reestablishing the administration as fast as could be expected under the circumstances. The checking framework that you worked in this section is a fine start for keeping framework proprietors mindful of prob-lems with a framework, however it does nothing to help reestablish administration.

At the point when every one of the procedures in a compartment has left, that holder will enter the left state. Keep in mind, a Docker holder can be in one of four states:
- Running
- Paused
- Restarting
- Exited (likewise utilized if the compartment has never been begun)

A fundamental procedure for recouping from brief disappointments is naturally restarting a procedure when it exits or fizzles. Docker gives a couple of alternatives to checking and restarting holders.

Automatically restarting containers

Docker furnishes this usefulness with a restart approach. Utilizing the - restart banner at holder creation time, you can advise Docker to do any of the accompanyings:
- never restart (default)
- Attempt to restart when a disappointment is identified
- Attempt for some foreordained time to restart when a disappointment is identified
- Always restart the compartment paying little heed to the condition

A docker doesn't generally endeavor to promptly restart a holder. On the off chance that it did, that would mess more up than it understood. Envision a compartment that sits idle however print the time and exit. On the off chance that that compartment was arranged to consistently restart and Docker in every case quickly restarted it, the framework would sit idle yet restart that holder. Rather, Docker utilizes an exponential backoff methodology for timing restart endeavors.

A backoff procedure decides how much time should go between progressive restart endeavors. An exponential backoff methodology will accomplish something like twofold the past time spent looking out for each progressive endeavor. For instance, if the first run through the compartment should be restarted Docker holds up 1 second, at that point on the second endeavor it would hold up 2 seconds, 4 seconds on the third endeavor, 8 on the fourth, etc. Exponential backoff systems with low introductory hold up times are a typical assistance reclamation method. You can see Docker utilize this methodology yourself by building a holder that consistently restarts and prints the time:

docker run - d - name backoff-indicator - restart consistently busybox date

At that point following a couple of moments, utilise the trailing logs highlight to watch it back off and restart:
docker logs - f backoff-indicator

The records will show every one of the occasions it has just been restarted and will hold up until whenever it is restarted, print the present time, and afterward exit. Adding this single banner to the observing framework and the WordPress holders you've been taking a shot at would explain the recuperation issue.

The main explanation you might not have any desire to embrace this straightforwardly is during backoff periods, and the compartment isn't running. Compartments holding back to be restarted are in the restarting state. To illustrate, attempt to run another procedure in the backoff-locator holder:

docker executive backoff-indicator reverberation Just a Test

Running that order should bring about a mistake message:

Can't run executive direction in the compartment: No dynamic holder exists with ID ...

That implies you can't do whatever requires the compartment to be running, as execute extra directions in the holder. That could be an issue on the off chance that you have to run symptomatic projects in a messed up holder. A progressively complete methodology is to utilize holders that init or boss forms.

A supervisor procedure, or init process, is a program that is utilized to dispatch and keep up the condition of different programs. On a Linux framework, PID #1 is an init procedure. It begins the various framework forms and restarts them if they bomb startlingly. It's a typical practice to utilize a comparable example inside containers to begin and oversee forms.

Utilizing a supervisor procedure inside your container will keep the container running if the objective procedure—a web server, for instance—fizzles and is restarted. There are a few projects that may be utilized inside a container. The most prevalent incorporate init, systemd, runit, upstart, and supervisord. For the time being, investigate a container that utilizations supervisord.

An organization named Tutum gives programming that delivers a full LAMP (Linux, Apache, MySQL PHP) stack inside a solitary container. Containers made along these lines use supervisord to ensure that all the related procedures are continued running. Start a model container:

docker run - d - p 80:80 - name light test tutum/light

You can perceive what procedures are running inside this container by utilizing the docker top direction:

docker top light test

The top subcommand will show the host PID for every one of the procedures in the con-tainer. You'll see supervisord, mysql, and apache remembered for the rundown of running genius grams. Since the container is running, you can test the supervisord restart usefulness by physically halting one of the procedures inside the container.

The issue is that to slaughter a procedure within a container from inside that container, you have to know the PID in the container's PID namespace. To get that rundown, run the accompanying executive subcommand:

docker executive light test ps

The procedure list produced will have recorded apache2 in the CMD segment:

PID TTY   TIME CMD

1 ?   00:00:00 supervisord

433 ?   00:00:00 mysqld_safe

835 ?   00:00:00 apache2

842 ?   00:00:00 ps

The qualities in the PID segment will be diverse when you run the order. Discover the

PID on the column for apache2 and afterward embed that for <PID> in the accompanying order:

docker executive light test murder <PID>

Running this direction will run the Linux slaughter program inside the light test container and advise the apache2 procedure to close down. When apache2 stops, the supervisord procedure will log the occasion and restart the procedure. The container logs will plainly show these occasions:

...

... left: apache2 (leave status 0; anticipated)

... brought forth: 'apache2' with pid 820

... achievement: apache2 entered RUNNING state, the process has kept awake for > than 1 second (startsecs)

A common alternative to using init or supervisor programs is to use a startup script that checks at least the prerequisites for running content software. Sometimes used as a default container command. For example, the WordPress repositories you created start executing the script to check and set the default environment variables before running the WordPress process. You can view this script by canceling the default command and using the command to view the contents of the run script:

docker runs wordpress: 4 cats /entrypoint.sh

Executing this command will generate error messages such as:
error: missing WORDPRESS_DB_HOST and MYSQL_PORT_3306_TCP environment
variables
...

This failed because, although you configured the command to run as cat /entrypoint.Sh, Docker containers execute what is known as an entry point before executing the command. Entry points are the perfect place to place code that confirms the prerequisites of the container. Although this is discussed in detail in Part 2 of this book, you need to know how to specifically replace or define a tank entry point on the command line. Try to execute the last command again, but this time uses the --entrypoint flag to specify the executable and use the command section to pass the arguments:

```
docker run --entrypoint = "cat" \
wordpress: 4 /entrypoint.sh
```

If you research the script shown, you will see how you validate environment variables according to software dependencies and set defaults. After the script confirms the execution of WordPress, run the requested or default command.

Boot scripts play an essential role in building durable containers and can always be combined with Docker restart strategies to reap the benefits of others. Because MySQL and WordPress repositories already use scripts to run, it is convenient to set a restart policy for each in an updated version of the sample script.

With this latest change, he created a complete WordPress web site provisioning system and learned the basics of container management using Docker.

A significant experiment. Your computer is probably full of containers that you no longer need. To restore the resources used by these containers, you must stop and remove them from your system.

Cleaning up

Ease of cleaning is one of the main reasons for using the cartridge and Docker. The isolation provided by the containers simplifies the steps to stop the process and delete the files. With Docker, the entire cleaning process comes down to one of several simple commands. In any cleaning task, you must first identify the container that you want to stop and dispose of. Remember to use the docker ps command to list all the containers on your computer:
docker ps - a

Since the containers you made for the models in this part won't be utilized once more, you ought to have the option to stop and expel all the recorded containers securely. Ensure you focus on the containers you're tidying up if there are any that you made for your very own exercises.

All containers use hard drive space to store logs, container metadata, and records that have been kept in touch with the container document framework. All containers likewise devour assets in the worldwide namespace like container names and host port mappings. By and large, containers that will never again be utilized ought to be evacuated.

To expel a container from your PC, utilize the docker rm command. For instance, to erase the halted container named wp you'd run:

docker rm wp

You ought to experience every one of the containers in the rundown you created by running docker ps - an and evacuate all containers that are in the left state. If you attempt to expel a container that is running, stopped, or restarting, Docker will show a message like the fol-lowing:

Error reaction from daemon: Conflict, You can't evacuate a running container. Stop the container before endeavoring evacuation or use - f

FATA[0000] Error: neglected to evacuate at least one containers

The procedures running in a container ought to be halted before the records in the container are evacuated. You can do this with the docker stop command or by utilizing the - f banner on docker rm. The key contrast is that when you stop a procedure utilizing the - f banner, Docker sends a SIG_KILL signal, which promptly ends the accepting procedure. Conversely, utilizing docker stop will send a SIG_HUP signal. Beneficiaries of SIG_HUP have the opportunity to perform conclusion and cleanup undertakings. The SIG_KILL signal offers for no such lenient gestures and can bring about record defilement or unfortunate system encounters. You can give a SIG_KILL straightforwardly to a container utilizing the docker murder command. Be that as it may, you should utilize docker kill or docker rm - f just if you should stop the container in under the standard 30-second most extreme stop time.

Later on, in case you're trying different things with fleeting containers, you can keep away from the cleanup trouble by determining - rm on the command. Doing so will naturally expel the container when it enters the left state. For instance, the accompanying command will compose a message to the screen in another BusyBox container, and the container will be evacuated when it exits:

docker run - rm - name auto-leave test busybox: latest reverberation Hello World
docker ps - a

For this situation, you could utilize either docker stop or docker rm to appropriately tidy up, or it is suitable to utilize the single-step docker rm - f command. You ought to likewise utilize the - v banner for reasons that will be shrouded in part 4. The docker CLI makes it is anything but difficult to create a speedy cleanup command:

docker rm - vf $(docker ps - a - q)

Summary

The essential focal point of the Docker venture is to empower clients to run programming in contain-ers. This section shows how you can utilize Docker for that reason. The thoughts and highlights secured incorporate the accompanying:

■ Containers can be run with virtual terminals appended to the client's shell or in segregated mode.

■ By default, each Docker container has its very own PID namespace, segregating process data for every container.

■ Docker recognizes each container by its created container ID, abridged container ID, or its human-accommodating name.

■ All containers are in any of four unmistakable states: running, delayed, restarting, or left.

■ The docker executive command can be utilized to run extra procedures inside a running container.

■ A client can pass enter or give extra design to a procedure in a container by indicating condition factors at a container-creation time.

■ Using the - read-just banner at container-creation time will mount the container record framework as read-just and forestall specialization of the container.

■ A container restart strategy, set with the - restart banner at container-creation time, will help your frameworks naturally recuperate in case of a disappointment.

■ Docker makes tidying up containers with the docker rm command as basic as making them.

Software installation simplified

We have presented every new idea and reflections gave by Docker. This part jumps further into container document frameworks and programming establishment. It separates programming establishment into three stages,

The initial phase in introducing any product is distinguishing the product you need to introduce. You realize that the product is dispersed utilizing pictures. However, you have to realize how to tell Docker precisely which picture you need to introduce. I've just referenced that archives hold pictures, yet in this part, I show

how stores and labels are utilised to identify pictures to introduce the product you need.

This section broadly expounds on the three fundamental approaches to introduce Docker pictures:

■ Docker Hub and different libraries

■ Using picture documents with docker spare and docker load

■ Building pictures with Dockerfiles

Throughout perusing this material, you'll figure out how Docker separates introduced the delicate product, and you'll be presented to another term, layer. Layers are a significant idea when managing pictures and importantly affect programming clients

Identifying software

Assume you need to introduce a program called TotallyAwesomeBlog 2.0. How might you disclose to Docker what you needed to introduce? You would require an approach to name the program, determine the adaptation that you need to utilize, and indicate the source that you need to introduce it from. Figuring out how to recognize explicit programming is the initial phase in programming establishment, You've discovered that Docker makes containers from pictures. A picture is a document. It holds records that will be accessible to containers made from it and metadata about the picture. This metadata contains data about connections between pictures, the com-mand history for a picture, uncovered ports, volume definitions, and that's just the beginning.

Pictures have identifiers, so they could be utilized as a name and form for the delicate product, however by and by it's uncommon to work with crude picture identifiers. They are long, exceptional groupings of letters and numbers. Every time a change is made to a picture, the picture identifier changes. Picture identifiers are hard to work with on the grounds that they're eccentric. Rather, clients work with storehouses.

What is a repository?

A repository is a named basin of pictures. The name is like a URL. A repository's name is comprised of the name of the host where the picture is found, the client account that possesses the picture, and a short name. For instance, later in this part, you will introduce a picture from the repository named quay.io/dockerinaction/ch3_hello_registry.

Similarly, as there can be a few adaptations of programming, a repository can hold a few pictures. Every one of the pictures in a repository is distinguished extraordinarily with tags. If I somehow happened to discharge another variant of quay.io/dockerinaction/ch3_hello_registry, I may label it "v2" while labeling the old adaptation with "v1." If you needed to download the old rendition, you could explicitly recognize that picture by its v1 tag.

You introduced a picture from the NGINX repository on Docker Hub that was related to the "most recent" tag. A repository name and label structure a composite key, or a special reference made up of a blend of non-novel segments. In that model, the picture was recognized by nginx: latest. Despite the fact that identifiers worked in this style may infrequently be longer than crude picture identifiers, they're unsurprising and convey the aim of the picture.

Utilizing tags

Tags are both a significant method to remarkably distinguish a picture and an advantageous method to make valuable monikers. While a tag must be applied to a solitary picture in a reposi-tory, a solitary picture can have a few tags. This enables repository proprietors to make use-ful forming or include tags.

For instance, the Java repository on Docker Hub keeps up the accompanying tags: 7, 7-jdk, 7u71, 7u71-jdk, openjdk-7, and openjdk-7u71. Every one of these tags is applied to a similar picture. In any case, as the present minor form of Java 7 increments, and they discharge 7u72, the 7u71 label will probably leave and be supplanted with 7u72. In the event that you care about what minor adaptation of Java 7 you're running, you need to stay aware of those label changes. In the event that you simply need to ensure you're continually running the latest variant of Java 7, simply utilize the picture labeled with 7. It will consistently be allocated to the most up to date minor update of Java 7. These tags give clients incredible adaptability.

It's additionally normal to see various tags for pictures with various programming configura-tions. For instance, I've discharged two pictures for an open source program called free-geoip. It's a web application that can be utilized to get the harsh land area related to a system address. One picture is designed to utilize the default configu-proportion for the product. It's intended to run without anyone else with an immediate connect to the world. The second is designed to run behind a web load balancer. Each picture has a particular label that enables the client to effectively recognize the picture with the highlights required.

TIP When you're searching for programming to introduce, consistently give cautious consideration to the tags offered in a repository. In case you don't know which one you need, you can download all the labeled pictures in a repository by just discarding the label qualifier when you pull from the repository. I incidentally do this unintentionally, and it very well may be irritating. Be that as it may, it's not difficult to tidy up.

This is everything to distinguishing programming for use with Docker. With this information, you're prepared to begin searching for and introducing programming with Docker.

Finding and installing software

You can identify the software by the name of the repository, but how do you find the repositories you want to install? Finding reliable software is complex, and the second step is learning how to install software with Docker.

To find repositories, keep guessing until you are lucky or use the index. Indexes are engines that catalog repositories. There are a lot of public Docker indexes, but by default, Docker is integrated into an index called the Docker Hub.

The Docker Hub is a registry and index of sites maintained by Docker Inc. This is the default registry and index that Docker uses. When you run a docker command or docker command without specifying a replacement record, Docker searches for storage in the Docker Hub by default. The Docker Hub makes Docker instantly more useful.

Docker Inc. worked to make Docker an open ecosystem. Post a public image to run your record, and the Docker command line tool can be easily configured to use other records. Other tools for installing and distributing images that came with Docker will be presented later in this chapter. But first, the following section explains how to utilize the default set of tools with Docker Hub fully.

Docker Hub from the command line

You can do nearly anything you can with Docker from the command line. This incorporates scanning for archives at the Docker Hub.

The Docker command will search the Docker Hub index and display results, including details such as the number of times each repository was submitted, an indicator indicating that a particular repository is official (the OFFICIAL column), and indicating whether the repository is what they call a trusted image (the TRUST column). The Docker Hub site allows registered users to create repositories similar to other community development sites such as GitHub. The number of stars in the repository can serve as a proxy metric to represent the quality and popularity of the image or the user's trust.

The Docker Hub also offers a suite of official repositories managed by Docker Inc. or current software maintainers. They are often called libraries.

An image author can publish his / her images in two ways at Docker Hub:

■ Use the command prompt to import images that you have created independently and on your system. Some find the images pushed this way less reliable because it is unclear how they were built.

■ Make the Docker file public and use the Docker Hub Continuous Compilation System. Dockerfiles are scripts for building images. Images created from these automatically linked versions are preferred because the Docker file is available for preview before installing the image. Images posted this way will be marked as trusted.

Working with private Docker Hub records or inserting them into records you manage in the Docker Hub requires authentication. In such a case, you can use the Docker login command to connect to the Docker Hub. Once logged in, you can extract private repositories, move to repositories that you control, and tag images in your repositories.

Running docker login will provoke you for your Docker Hub certifications. When you've given them, your command-line customer will be verified, and you'll have the option to get to your private archives. At the point when you've got done with working with your record, you can log out with the docker logout command.

If you need to discover programming to introduce, you'll have to realize where to start your inquiry. The following model exhibits how to look for stores utilizing the docker search command. This command may take a couple of moments. However, it has a break inherent, so it will in the end return. At the point when you run this command, it will just look through the file; nothing will be introduced.

Assume Bob, a product designer, chose that the task he was chipping away at required a database. He had found out about a well known program named Postgres. He thought about whether it was accessible on Docker Hub, so he ran the accompanying command:

docker search postgres

Following a few moments, a few results were returned. At the highest priority on the rundown, he distinguished a common repository with many stars. He additionally preferred that it was an official repository, which implied that the Docker Hub maintainers had painstakingly chosen the proprietors of the repository. He utilized docker dismantle to introduce the picture and proceeded onward with his undertaking.

This is a straightforward case of how to look for archives utilizing the docker command line. The command will scan Docker Hub for any archives with the term postgres. Since Docker Hub is a free open assistance, clients will, in general, develop heaps of open, however close to home duplicates. Docker Hub gives clients a chance to star a repository, like a Facebook Like. This is a sensible intermediary marker for picture quality, however you ought to be mindful so as not to utilize it as a pointer of dependable code.

Suppose somebody develops a repository with a few hundred stars by giving some excellent open source programming. One day a vindictive programmer oversees their repository and distributes a picture to the repository that contains an infection. In spite of the fact that containers may be viable for containing malevolent code, that thought doesn't remain constant for pernicious pictures. On the off chance that an aggressor controls how a picture is fabricated or has focused on an assault explicitly to break out of a debilitated picture, a picture can cause genuine mischief. Consequently, pictures that are constructed utilizing openly accessible contents are viewed as substantially more reliable. In the indexed lists from running docker search, you can tell that a picture was worked from an open content by searching for an [OK] in the section mark AUTOMATED.

Presently you've perceived how to discover programming on Docker Hub without leaving your terminal. Even though you can accomplish most things from the terminal, there are a few things that you can do just through the site.

Docker Hub from the site

If you presently can't seem to unearth it while perusing docker.com, you should pause for a minute to look at *https://hub.docker.com*. Docker Hub gives you a chance to look for vaults, associations, or explicit clients. Client and association profile pages list the storehouses that the record keeps up, ongoing action on the record, and the archives that the record has featured. On repository pages you can see the accompanying:

■ General data about the picture gave by the picture distributer

■ A rundown of the tags accessible in the repository

■ The date the repository was made

■ How many times it has been downloaded

■ Any comment from enrolled clients

To utilize the projects in these pictures, you'll have to join your terminal to the containers with the goal that the information and yield of your terminal are associated straightforwardly to the running container. The accompanying command exhibits how to do that and run a container that will be evacuated consequently when halted:

docker run - it - rm dockerinaction/ch3_ex2_hunt

At the point when you run this command, the forager chase program will incite you for the password. On the off chance that you know the appropriate response as of now, feel free to enter it now. If not, enter anything, and it will give you an indication. Now, you ought to have every one of the apparatuses you have to complete the action.

At the point when you find the solution, pat yourself on the back and evacuate the pictures utilising the docker rmi command. Solidly, the codes you run will look something like these:

docker rmi dockerinaction/ch3_ex2_hunt
docker rmi <mystery repository>

On the off chance that you were following the models and utilizing the - rm choice on your docker run commands, you ought to have no containers to tidy up. You've taken in a great deal in this model. You've discovered another picture on Docker Hub and utilized the docker run command in another manner. There's a great deal to think about running intelligent containers. The following segment covers that in more noteworthy detail.

Docker Hub is in no way, shape or forms the primary hotspot for programming. Contingent upon the objectives and viewpoint of programming distributers, Docker Hub may not be a fitting circulation point. Shut source or exclusive ventures might not have any desire to chance to distribute their product through an outsider. There are three different approaches to introduce the product:

■ You can utilize elective repository vaults or run your very own library.

■ You can physically stack pictures from a document.

■ You can download a venture from some other source and fabricate a picture utilizing a gave Dockerfile.

Every one of the three of these choices is reasonable for private ventures or corporate framework.

The following hardly any subsections spread how to introduce programming from every elective source.

Using alternative registries

As referenced before, Docker makes the library programming accessible for anybody to run. Facilitating organizations have incorporated it into their contributions, and organizations have started running their very own inner libraries.

I'm not going to cover running a vault, yet it's significant that you figure out how to utilize them early.

Utilizing an elective vault is straightforward. It requires no extra design. All you need is the location of the library. The accompanying command will download another "Welcome World" type model from an elective library:

docker pull quay.io/dockerinaction/ch4_hello_registry:latest

The library address is a piece of the full repository detail

The full example is as per the following:

[REGISTRYHOST/][USERNAME/]NAME[: TAG]

Docker realizes how to converse with Docker libraries, so the main contrast is that you indicate the vault have. Now and again, working with libraries will require a confirmation step. At the point when you're done with the welcome library picture you introduced, expel it with the accompanying command:

docker rmi quay.io/dockerinaction/ch4_hello_registry

Libraries are incredible. They empower a client to give up control of picture stockpiling and transportation. In any case, running your very own vault can be convoluted and may make a potential single purpose of a disappointment for your arrangement framework. In the event that running a custom library sounds somewhat confused for your utilization case, and outsider appropriation apparatuses are impossible, you should think about stacking pictures straightforwardly from a document.

Pictures as records

Docker gives a command to stack pictures into Docker from a document. With this apparatus, you can stack pictures that you gained through different channels. Perhaps your organization has decided to convey pictures through a focal record server or some form control framework. Possibly the picture is little enough that your companion sent it to you over email or shared it by means of glimmer drive. Anyway, you happened upon the document, and you can stack it into Docker with the docker load command.

You'll require a picture record to stack before I can show you the docker load command. Since it's far-fetched that you have a picture document lying around, I'll tell you the best way to spare one from a stacked picture. For the reasons for this model, you'll pull busybox: latest. That picture is little and simple to work with. To spare that picture to a document, utilize the docker spare command.

I utilized the .tar filename postfix in this model because the docker spare command makes TAR file documents. You can utilize any filename you need. On the off chance that you miss the – o banner, the subsequent record will be gushed to the terminal.

Layer relationships

Images maintain parent/child connections. In these connections, they work from their folks and structure layers. The documents accessible to a container are the association of the entirety of the layers in the lineage of the picture the container was created from. Images can have associations with some other picture, including images in different repositories with different proprietors.

The layers are an example of the java:6 picture at the hour of this writing. A picture is named when its creator labels and distributes it. A client can create pseudonyms, as you did prior using the docker label command. Until a picture is labeled, the best way to allude to it is to utilize its remarkable identifier (UID) that was produced when the picture was constructed. The guardians of the regular Java 6 picture are marked using the initial 12 digits of their UID. These layers contain basic libraries and conditions of the Java 6 programming. Docker truncates the UID from 65 (base 16) digits to 12 to serve its human clients. Internally and through API get to, Docker utilizes the full 65. It's essential to know about this when you've installed images alongside comparable anonymous images. I wouldn't need you to think something terrible occurred or some vindictive programming had made it into your PC when you see these images included when you utilize the docker images command.

The Java images are sizable. At the hour of this writing, the openjdk-6 picture is 348 MB, and the openjdk-7 picture is 590 MB. You get some space savings when you utilize the runtime-just images, yet even openjre-6 is 200 MB. Again, Java was picked here in light of the fact that its images are especially enormous for a typical reliance.

Container file system abstraction and isolation

Projects that run in containers don't think about the layers of the image. Inside the container, the file system functions as if it were not working on the container or image. From a tank standpoint, it contains restrictive copies of the files the image contains. This becomes conceivable with what is called the join file system. Docker uses a variety of file systems to join and will choose the one that best suits your system. The complexities of how a file association system works have overcome what you need to know to use Docker successfully.

An association file system is an element of a set of basic instruments that combine to create a powerful separation of file systems. Different devices are DTM namespaces and chroot system call.

The file system is used to create mount points in your host file system that conceptualize the use of layers. The layers created are what is packed into the Docker image layers. Similarly, when a Docker image is installed, its layers are downloaded and properly organized for use by the file system provider selected for your system.

The Linux part gives the DTM system a namespace. When Docker creates a container, this new container will have its own MNT namespace, and a second mount point will be created for the container in the image.

In conclusion, chroot is used to make the database of the image file system the root of the unique circumstances of the container. This prevents any item contained in the container from referencing another item in the host file system.

Using chroot and DTM namespaces is necessary to improve the container. When adding a file system to join a formula, Docker containers have some advantages.

Advantages of this toolset and file system structure

The first and perhaps most important advantage of this methodology is that it is basic

The layers must be installed once. If you install an unlimited number of images and they all depend on the standard layer, that base layer and all its main layers must be downloaded or installed once. This implies that you can install some of the program specializations without storing excess files on your computer or downloading repetitive layers. Most advances in virtual machines, on the other hand, store files that are indistinguishable, usually when you have repetitive virtual machines on your computer.

Second, diapers provide a rude way of handling conditions and difficulties separately. This is especially useful for software developers. From a customer standpoint, this benefit will help you quickly sort out the software you use when examining the images and layers you use.

Finally, it is very difficult to create software specializations when small changes can be made to the basic image. Giving specific images helps customers get exactly what they need from the software with minimal customization. This is probably the best motivation to use Docker.

Shortcomings of union file systems

Docker will pick the best file system for the system it's running on. However, no imple-mentation is ideal for each remaining task at hand. Truth be told, there are some particular use situations when you should delay and consider utilizing another Docker highlight.

Different file systems have different properties depending on the properties, size, filenames and characters. Union file systems find themselves often having to interpret the principles of different file systems. At best, they are prepared to provide adequate interpretations. In most pessimistic scenarios, forces are ignored. For example, neither btrfs nor OverlayFS help with the global properties that make SELinux work.

Union file systems use an example called duplicate on-compose, and that makes actualize ing memory-mapped files (the mmap() system call) troublesome. Some union file systems
give usage that works under the correct conditions, yet it might be a superior plan to stay away from memory-mapping files from a picture.

The support file system is another pluggable element of Docker. You can figure out which file system your establishment is utilizing with the information subcommand. In case you need to explicitly reveal to Docker the file system you will use, do so as such with the capacity manager of your choice, or - with when you launch the Docker daemon. You can solve most problems related to maintaining a syndicated file system without changing the capacity provider. This can be understood by volumes

Summary
The errand of introducing and overseeing software on a PC shows a one of a kind arrangement of difficulties. This part clarifies how you can utilize Docker to address them. The center thoughts and highlights secured by this part are as per the following:

■   Human Docker clients use vault names to impart which software they might want Docker to introduce.

■   Docker Hub is the default Docker library. You can discover software on Docker Hub through either the site or the docker command-line program.

■   The docker command-line program makes it easy to introduce software that is conveyed through elective libraries or in different structures.

■   The picture archive particular incorporates a vault have field.

■   The docker burden and docker spare commands can be utilized to load and spare images from TAR documents.

■   Distributing a Dockerfile with a task improves picture expands on client machines.

■   Images are typically identified with different images in parent/youngster connections. These connections structure layers. At the point when we state that we have introduced a picture, we are stating that we have introduced an objective picture and each picture layer in its genealogy.

Organizing images with layers empowers layer reuse and spares bandwidth during dispersion and extra room on your PC.

Did you see it? Unless your network connection is far better than mine, or you had already installed Java 6 as a dependency of some other image, the download for dockerinaction/ch3_myapp should have been much slower than dockerinaction/ch3_myotherapp.

When you installed ch3_myapp, Docker determined that it needed to install the openjdk-6 image because it's the direct dependency (parent layer) of the requested image. When Docker went to install that dependency, it discovered the dependencies of that layer and downloaded those first. Once all the dependencies of a layer are installed, that layer is installed. Finally, openjdk-6 was installed, and then the tiny ch3_myapp layer was installed.

When you issued the command to install ch3_myotherapp, Docker identified that openjdk-6 was already installed and immediately installed the image for ch3_myotherapp. This was simpler, and because less than one megabyte of data was transferred, it was faster. But again, to the user, it was an identical process.

From the user perspective, this ability is nice to have, but you wouldn't want to have to try to optimize for it. Just take the benefits where they happen to work out. From the perspective of a software or image author, this ability should play a major factor in your image design.

If you run docker images now, you'll see the following repositories listed:

> dockerinaction/ch3_myapp

> dockerinaction/ch3_myotherapp

> java:6

By default, the docker images command will only show you repositories. Similar to other commands, if you specify the -a flag, the list will include every installed interme-diate image or layer. Running docker images -a will show a list that includes several repositories listed as <none>. The only way to refer to these is to use the value in the IMAGE ID column.

In this example, you installed two images directly, but a third parent repository was installed as well. You'll need to clean up all three. You can do so more easily if you use the condensed docker rmi syntax:

docker rmi \

dockerinaction/ch3_myapp \

dockerinaction/ch3_myotherapp \

java:6

The docker rmi command allows you to specify a space-separated list of images to be removed. This comes in handy when you need to remove a small set of images after an example. I'll be using this when appropriate throughout the rest of the examples in this book.

Persistent storage and shared state with volumes

At this point in the book, you've installed and run a few programs. You've seen some examples of toys, but haven't seen anything that resembles the real world. This chapter presents the quantities of Docker Volume and the strategies you will use to manage your container data.

Think about what it would be like to run a database program in a container. You can also package software with an image at the beginning of the container,

You can initialize an empty database. When programs connect to a database and enter data, where are they stored? Is it in a file inside the container? What happens to this information when you stop the tank or delete it? How would you move your data if you wanted to update a database program?

Imagine another situation where you run different web applications in different containers. Where would you write the log files to survive the tank? How would you access these records to resolve the issue? How can other programs, such as the registration summary tool, access these files? The answer to all these questions involves the use of volumes.

Presentation of volumes.

A set of mount points creates a directory tree of the host or container that describes how to assemble one or more file systems. Volume is the mount point for the container tree where part of the computer directory tree is mounted. Most people know very little about file systems and mount points and rarely adjust them. People have more difficulty with volumes than with any other Docker topic. The lack of knowledge of editing points contributes to the factor.

Without volume, container users are limited to working with a union file system that provides image images. The first file is written to the root file system. The operating system sends changes from the root file system to the top layer of the mounted Union file system. The second file is written to the volume that is embedded in the u / data container directory tree. This change is made directly to the host file system via volume.

Although a union file system works to create and share images, it is far from ideal for working with permanent or shared data. Quantities meet these use cases and play a vital role in container design.

The quantities allow the container data to be managed independently

Semantically, volume is a segmentation and data sharing tool with scope or lifecycle independent of a single container. This is why volumes are an important part of any designed system container that shares or writes files. The following are examples of data whose range or access is different from the container:

■ Database and database software.

■ Web application versus registration information

■ Data processing application with respect to input and output data

■ Web server versus static content

■ Products versus support tools

Quantities help to separate problems and create modularity in architectural components. This modularity helps you to understand, create, support and reuse more important parts of the system more easily.

Think of it this way: images are suitable for packing and distributing relatively static files, such as programs; The volumes contain dynamic data or specializations. This difference makes it possible to share reusable images and easy data. This separation of relatively static and dynamic file space allows application or image authors to implement advanced models as polymorphic and composting tools.

A polymorphic instrument is one that keeps up a predictable interface yet may have a few executions that accomplish various things. Consider an application, for example, a general application server. Apache Tomcat, for instance, is an application that gives a HTTP interface on a system and dispatches any solicitations it gets to pluggable projects. Tomcat has polymorphic conduct. Utilizing volumes, you can infuse conduct into containers without altering a picture. Then again, consider a database ace gram like MongoDB or MySQL. The estimation of a database is characterized by the information it contains. A database program consistently shows a similar interface yet takes on an entirely extraordinary worth relying upon the information that can be infused with a volume. The polymorphic container design is the subject of area.

All the more generally, volumes empower the division of utilization and host concerns. Sooner or later a picture will be stacked onto a host and a container made from it. Docker thinks minimal about the host where it's running and can just make statements about what documents ought to be accessible to a container. That implies Docker alone has no real way to exploit have explicit offices like mounted system stockpiling or blended turning and strong state hard drives. Yet, a client with information on the host can utilize volumes to delineate in a container to fitting stockpiling on that host.

Presently that you're comfortable with what volumes are and for what reason they're significant, you can begin with them in a true model.

Utilizing volumes with a NoSQL database

The Apache Cassandra venture gives a section database worked in grouping, possible consistency, and direct compose adaptability. It's a mainstream decision in present day framework structures, and an official picture is accessible on Docker Hub. Cassandra resembles different databases in that it stores its information in records on plate. In this area you'll utilize the official Cassandra picture to make a solitary hub Cassandra group, make a keyspace, erase the container, and afterward recuperate that keyspace on another hub in another container.

Begin by making a solitary container that characterizes a volume. This is known as a volume container. Volume containers are one of the propelled examples talked about later in this part:

```
docker run -d \
- volume/var/lib/cassandra/information \
- Name cass-shared \
Alpine echo Data Container
```

The volume container will quickly stop. That is suitable for this model. Try not to expel it yet. You're going to utilize the volume it made when you make another container running Cassandra:

```
docker run -d \
- Volumes-from cass-shared \
- name cass1 \
Cassandra: 2.2
```

After Docker pulls the cassandra:2.2 picture from Docker Hub, it makes another container and duplicates the volume definitions from the volume container. From that point onward, the two containers have a volume mounted at/var/lib/cassandra/information that focuses to a similar area on the host's catalog tree. Next, start a container from the cassandra:2.2 picture, however run a Cassandra customer device and associate with your running server:

```
docker run – it - rm \
- interface cass1:cass \
cassandra:2.2 cqlsh cass
```

Presently you can review or change your Cassandra database from the CQLSH command line. To begin with, search for a keyspace named docker_hello_world:

```
select *
From system.schema_keyspaces
Where keyspace_name = 'docker_hello_world';
```

Cassandra should restore an unfilled rundown. This implies the database hasn't been changed by the model. Next, make that keyspace with the accompanying command:

```
make keyspace docker_hello_world
with replication = {
'class' : 'SimpleStrategy',
'replication_factor': 1
};
```

Since you've altered the database, you ought to have the option to give a similar question again to see the outcomes and check that your progressions were acknowledged. The accompanying command is equivalent to the one you ran before:

```
select *
from system.schema_keyspaces
where keyspace_name = 'docker_hello_world';
```

This time Cassandra should restore a solitary section with the properties you determined when you made the keyspace. In case you're fulfilled that you've associated with and modified your Cassandra hub, quit the CQLSH program to stop the customer container:

```
# Leave and stop the present container quit
```

The customer container was made with the - rm banner and was consequently expelled when the command halted. Keep tidying up the initial segment of this model by halting and evacuating the Cassandra hub you made:

```
docker stop cass1
docker rm - vf cass1
```

The client and Cassandra server you created will be deleted after executing these commands. If the changes you make persist, the only place I can stay is the volume container. If true, the scope of this data has expanded to two containers, and its life cycle has extended beyond the container in which the data was created.

You can try this by repeating these steps. Create a new Cassandra node, connect the client, and find the key space.

The following three commands will test your data recovery:

```
docker run -d \
--volumes-from cass-shared \
--name cass2 \
cassandra:2.2

docker run –it --rm \
--link cass2:cass \
cassandra:2.2 \
cqlsh cass

select *
from system.schema_keyspaces
where keyspace_name = 'docker_hello_world';
```

The last direction in this set returns a solitary passage, and it coordinates the keyspace you made in the past holder. This affirms the past cases and exhibits how volumes may be utilized to make tough frameworks. Before proceeding onward, quit the CQLSH program and tidy up your workspace. Try to evacuate that volume holder too:

```
quit
docker rm - vf cass2 cass-shared
```

This model shows one approach to utilize volumes without going into how they work, the examples being used, or how to oversee volume life cycle. The rest of this chap-ter jumps further into every feature of volumes, beginning with the various types accessible.

Volume types

There are two types of volume. Each volume is a mount point on the holder registry tree to an area on the host catalog tree, yet the types vary in where that area is on the host. The main sort of volume is a bind mount. Bind mount volumes utilize any client determined catalog or record on the host working framework. The subsequent sort is an overseen volume. Overseen volumes use areas that are made by the Docker daemon in space constrained by the daemon, called Docker oversaw space.

Each sort of volume has preferences and inconveniences. Contingent upon your particular use case, you may need to utilize one or be not able utilize the other. This area investigates each type top to bottom.

A bind mount volume is a volume that focuses to a client indicated area on the host document framework. Bind mount volumes are valuable when the host gives some record or index that should be mounted into the holder registry tree at a particular point

Bind mount volumes are helpful in the event that you need to impart information to different procedures running outside a compartment, for example, parts of the host framework itself. They likewise work on the off chance that you need to share information that lives on your host at some known area with a particular ace gram that runs in a holder.

For instance, assume you're taking a shot at an archive or website page on your neighborhood PC and need to impart your work to a companion. One approach to do so is to use Docker to dispatch a web server and serve content that you've duplicated into the web server picture. In spite of the fact that that would work and may even be a best practice for produc-tion situations, it's bulky to remake the picture each time you need to share a refreshed form of the archive.

Rather, you could utilize Docker to dispatch the web server and bind mount the loca-tion of your record into the new holder at the web server's report root. You can attempt this for yourself. Make another catalog in your home index called test ple-docs. Presently make a record named index.html in that catalog. Include a decent message for your companion to the record. The accompanying order will begin an Apache HTTP server where your new index is bind mounted to the server's archive root:

```
docker run - d - name bmweb \
- v ~/model docs:/usr/nearby/apache2/htdocs \
- p 80:80 \
httpd:latest
```

With this compartment running, you ought to have the option to point your internet browser at the IP address where your Docker motor is running and see the document you made.

In this model you utilized the - v choice and an area guide to make the bind mount volume. The guide is delimited with a colon (as is basic with Linux-style order line instruments). The guide key (the way before the colon) is the supreme way of an area on the host record framework, and the worth (the way after the colon) is where it ought to be mounted inside the compartment. You should determine areas with outright ways.

This model addresses a significant quality or highlight of volumes. At the point when you mount a volume on a holder record framework, it replaces the substance that the picture professional vides at that area. In this model, the httpd:latest picture gives some default HTML content at/usr/neighborhood/apache2/htdocs/, yet when you mounted a volume at that area, the substance gave by the picture was superseded by the substance on the host. This conduct is the reason for the polymorphic holder design examined later in the part.

Developing this utilization case, assume you need to ensure that the Apache HTTP web server can't change the substance of this volume. Indeed, even the most believed programming can contain vulnerabilities, and it's ideal to limit the effect of an assault on your site. Luckily, Docker gives an instrument to mount volumes as read-in particular. You can do this by annexing :ro to the volume map detail. In the model, you should change the run command to something like the accompanying:

docker rm - vf bmweb
docker run - name bmweb_ro \
- volume ~/model docs:/usr/neighborhood/apache2/htdocs/:ro \
- p 80:80 \
httpd:latest

By mounting the volume as read-no one but, you can avoid any procedure inside the con-tainer from adjusting the substance of the volume. You can see this in real life by running a speedy test:

docker run - rm \
- v ~/model docs:/testspace:ro \
high \
/canister/sh - c 'reverberation test >/testspace/test'

This command begins a holder with a comparative read-just bind mounts as the web server. It runs a command that attempts to add the word test to a document named test in the volume. The command comes up short because the volume is mounted as read-as it was.

At last, note that if you indicate a host registry that doesn't exist, Docker will make it for you. Even though this can prove to be useful, depending on this usefulness isn't the best idea. It's better to have more control over the ownership and permissions set on a directory.

ls ~/example-docs/absent

```
docker run --rm -v ~/example-docs/absent:/absent alpine:latest \

/bin/sh -c 'mount | grep absent'

ls ~/example-docs/absent
```

Bind mount volumes aren't restricted to indexes, however that is the way they're every now and again utilized. You can utilize bind mount volumes to mount singular records. This gives the adaptability to make or connection assets at a level that maintains a strategic distance from strife with different assets. Think about when you need to mount a particular record into an index that contains different documents. Solidly, assume you just needed to serve a solitary extra document close by the web content that dispatched with some pictures. In the event that you utilize a bind mount of an entire registry over that area, different documents will be lost. By utilizing a particular record as a volume, you can abrogate or infuse singular documents.

The significant thing to note for this situation is that the record must exist on the host before you make the compartment. Something else, Docker will accept that you needed to utilize an index, make it on the host, and mount it at the ideal area (regardless of whether that area is involved by a record).

The primary issue with bind mount volumes is that they tie generally compact compartment depictions to the document arrangement of a particular host. In the event that a holder portrayal relies upon content at a particular area on the host document framework, at that point that depiction isn't convenient to have where the substance is inaccessible or accessible in some other area.

The following enormous issue is that they make an open door to struggle with different holders. It would be an ill-conceived notion to begin numerous occasions of Cassandra that all utilization a similar host area as a volume. Every one of the cases would vie for a similar arrangement of records. Without different devices, for example, record bolts, that would almost certainly bring about the defilement of the database.

Bind mount volumes are suitable apparatuses for workstations or machines with specific concerns. It's smarter to maintain a strategic distance from these sorts of explicit bindings in summed up stages or equipment pools. You can exploit volumes in a host-freethinker and compact path with Docker-oversaw volumes.

Docker-managed volumes

Overseen volumes are unique in relation to binding mount volumes because the Docker daemon makes oversaw volumes in a segment of the host's record framework that is possessed by Docker. Utilizing oversaw volumes is a technique for decoupling volumes from specific areas on the document framework.

Overseen volumes are made when you utilize the - v alternative (or - volume) on docker run yet determine the mount point in the compartment catalog tree.

You made an oversaw volume in the Cassandra The compartment named cass-shared indicated a volume at/var/lib/cassandra/information:

```
docker
run
-d \

-v
/var/lib/cassandra/data \

--name
cass-shared \

alpine
echo Data Container
```

When you created this container, the Docker daemon created directories to store the contents of the three volumes somewhere in the part of the host file system that it controls. To find out exactly where this folder is, you can use the filtered command to check the docked window for the Volumes key. The important thing to remove from this result is that Docker created each of the volumes in the directory managed by the host Docker daemon:

```
docker view -f "{{json .Volumes}}" cass-shared
```

The inspection subcommand will generate a list of mount points for the container and the corresponding path in the computer directory tree. The output will look like this:

```
{"/ var / lib / cassandra / data": "/ mnt / sda1 / var / lib / docker / vfs / dir / 632fa59c ..."}
```

The volume key indicates a value that is the map itself. In this folder, each key is a mount point in the container, and the value is the location of the directory in the host file system. Here we are reviewing the volume container. The card is sorted according to the lexicographic order of their keys and is independent of the order given when creating the container.

TIP (Docker Machine or Boot2Docker) should keep in mind that the host path is specified in each value relative to the root file system of their virtual machine, not the host root. Managed volumes are created on a machine running the Docker daemon, but VirtualBox will create link mounting volumes that refer to directories or files on the host computer.

The quantities that manage Docker may seem difficult to use if you manually assemble or connect tools on your desktop, but on larger systems where a particular data location is less important, managed volumes are a much more efficient way of organizing data. , Its use separates all other potential problems with the system. With volumes managed by Docker, it simply says, "I need a place to store some of the data I work with." The point is that Docker can charge all the machines on which Docker is installed. Also, when you finish the volume and ask Docker to clean up all the stuff for you, Docker can confidently delete any directory or file that the container no longer uses. Using volume this way helps to control congestion. As middleware or Docker add-ons develop, users of managed volumes will be able to adopt more advanced features, such as portable volumes.

Sharing access to data is a key feature of volume. If you have partitioned known bundles of files in the file system, you should know how to split a volume between containers without exposing the exact

location of the managed containers. The following section describes two ways to share data between containers using volume.

Sharing volumes

Suppose you have a web server running in the container that records all requests you receive in / logs / access. If you want to move these records from your web server to more permanent storage, you can do so with a script in a different container. The amounts of exchange between the tanks are areas where their value becomes more apparent. Just as there are two types of volume, there are two ways of dividing volume between containers.

Sharing depends on the host

You've already read about the tools needed to implement host-dependent sharing. It is said that two or more containers use a host-dependent share when each has a link mount volume for one known location in the host file system. This is the most obvious way of dividing disk space between containers.

In this example, you created two containers: one is called a plath that writes rows to a file and another that shows the top of a file. These containers share the total connection embedding volume. Outside of any container, you can see changes by adding the contents of the directory you created or by viewing a new file.

Explore how containers can be interconnected in this way. The following example starts with four containers: two registers and two units:

```
docker run --name woolf -d \
--volume ~/web-logs-example:/data \
dockerinaction/ch4_writer_a
docker run --name alcott -d \
-v ~/web-logs-example:/data \
dockerinaction/ch4_writer_b
docker run --rm --entrypoint head \
-v ~/web-logs-example:/towatch:ro \
alpine:latest \
/towatch/logA
docker run --rm \
-v ~/web-logs-example:/toread:ro \
alpine:latest \
head /toread/logB
```

In this example, he created four containers, each of which contained the same directory as the volume. The first two containers are written to different files in this volume. The third and fourth tanks raise the volume to second and read only. This example is a toy, but it clearly demonstrates a feature that could be useful given the variety of ways people build images and software.

Host-dependent sharing requires the use of link mount volumes, but for related reasons, host-dependent sharing can cause problems or be too expensive to manage if you work with a large number of hosts. machines. The following section provides a shortcut to share managed volumes and link assembly volumes to a set of containers.

General sharing and bookmarking

The run docker command provides an indicator that copies the volumes of one or more containers to a new container. The --volumes-from flag can be configured several times to specify multiple source containers.

Using this metric, he copied the managed volume defined by the volume container into each container running Cassandra. The example is realistic but does not allow to illustrate some specific container behaviors - volumes - from and managed container:

```
docker run - fowler name \
-v ~ / copies: library / PoEAA \
-v / library / DSL \
```

```
Alpine: last \
echo "Fowler Collection created".
docker run - name knuth \
-v /library/TAoCP.vol1 \
-v /library/TAoCP.vol2 \
-v /library/TAoCP.vol3 \
-v /library/TAoCP.vol4.a \
Alpine: last \
echo "Knuth Collection Created"
  --volumes-from fowler \
  --volumes-from knuth \
  alpine:latest ls -l /library/
  docker inspect --format "{{json .Volumes}}" reader
```

In this example, you created two containers that define volumes managed by Docker as well as the volume of connection mounting. Share them with a third container with no label - of volume, you need to inspect previously created containers and and then associate mounting links to host directories managed by Docker. Docker knows all in his name when he uses the flag - notebooks-of. Copy any volume present in the original container specified in the new container. In this case a tainer called drive copied all volumes defined by fowler and knuth.

You can copy quantities directly or transiently. This means that if you copy. volumes from another container will also copy volumes copied from specific files.

Other containers The use of tanks created in the last example generates the following:

docker run - name aggregator \ - volumes-from fowler \ - volumes-from knuth \ alpine:latest \

reverberation "Assortment Created."

docker run - rm \

- volumes-from aggregator \

alpine:latest \

ls - l/library/

Replicated volumes consistently have a similar mount point. That implies that you can't utilize - volumes-from in three circumstances.

In the principal circumstance, you can't utilize - volumes-from if the holder you're fabricate ing needs a mutual volume mounted to an alternate area. It offers no tooling for remapping mount focuses. It will just duplicate and association the mount focuses determined by the predetermined holders. For instance, if the understudy in the last model needed to mount the library to an area like/school/library, they wouldn't have the option to do as such.

The subsequent circumstance happens when the volume sources strife with one another or another volume particular. Sources make an oversaw volume with a similar mount point, at that point a customer of both will get just one of the volume definitions:

docker run - name chomsky - volume/library/ss \ alpine:latest reverberation "Chomsky assortment made."

docker run - name lamport - volume/library/ss \ alpine:latest reverberation "Lamport assortment made."

docker run - name understudy \

- volumes-from chomsky - volumes-from lamport \ alpine:latest ls - l/library/

docker investigate - f "" understudy

Now when you run the model, the yield of docker investigate will show that the last con-tainer has just a solitary volume recorded at/library/ss and its worth is equivalent to one of the other two. Each source holder characterises a similar mount point, and you make a race condition by replicating both to the new compartment. Just one of the two duplicate drama tions can succeed.

A true model where this would restrain is on the off chance that you were replicating the volumes of a few web servers into a solitary holder for review. On the off chance that those servers are on the whole running similar programming or offer basic arrangement (which is almost certainly in a containerised framework), at that point every one of those servers may utilize a similar mount focuses. All things considered, the mount focuses would strife, and you'd have the option to get to just a subset of the necessary information.

The third circumstance where you can't utilize - volumes-from is in the event that you have to change the compose authorization of a volume. This is on the grounds that - volumes-from duplicates the definition of the full volume. For instance, if your source has a volume mounted with read/compose access, and you need to impart that to a compartment that ought to have just understood access, utilizing - volumes-from won't work.

Imparting volumes to the - volumes-from banner is a significant apparatus for building convenient application designs, yet it introduces a few constraints. Utilizing Docker-oversaw volumes decouples holders from the information and document framework struc-ture of the host machine, and that is basic for most creation conditions. The records and catalogs that Docker makes for oversaw volumes still should be represented and kept up. To see how Docker functions with these documents and how to keep your Docker condition clean, you have to comprehend the overseen volume life cycle.

The oversaw volume life cycle

By this point in the section you ought to have quite a couple of holders and volumes to tidy up. I've precluded cleanup guidelines so far so you have an abundance of mate-rial to use in this segment. Overseen volumes have life cycles that are free of any compartment, yet as of this keeping in touch with you can just reference them by the holders that utilization them.

Volume possession

Overseen volumes are inferior elements. You have no real way to share or erase a particular oversaw volume since you have no real way to distinguish an oversaw volume.

Overseen volumes are possibly made when you preclude a bind mount source, and they're just recognizable by the holders that utilization them.

The most noteworthy devotion approach to distinguish volumes is to characterize a solitary compartment for each oversaw volume. In doing as such, you can be quite certain about which volumes you con-sume. All the more significantly, doing so encourages you to erase explicit volumes. Except if you resort to inspecting volume mappings on a compartment and physically tidying up the Docker-oversaw space, evacuating volumes requires a referencing holder, and that makes it imperative to comprehend which compartments claim each oversaw volume.

A holder possesses all oversaw volumes mounted to its record framework, and numerous compartments can claim a volume like in the fowler, knuth, and peruser model. Docker tracks these references on oversaw volumes to guarantee that no as of now referenced volume is erased.

Tidying up volumes

Tidying up oversaw volumes is a manual undertaking. This default usefulness forestalls unplanned pulverisation of possibly significant information. Docker can't erase bind mount volumes because the source exists outside the Docker scope. Doing so could bring about all way of contentions, shakiness, and inadvertent information misfortune.

Docker can erase oversaw volumes while erasing holders. Running the docker rm command with the - v alternative will endeavor to erase any oversaw volumes referenced by the objective compartment. Any oversaw volumes that are referenced by different compartments will be skipped; however, the inward counters will be decremented. This is a protected default, yet it can prompt the dangerous situation

On the off chance that you erase each compartment that references an oversaw volume yet neglect to utilize the - v banner, you'll make that volume a vagrant. Expelling stranded volumes requires untidy manual advances, however relying upon the size of the volumes it might merit the exertion. Then again, there are vagrant volume cleanup contents that you should seriously mull over utilizing. You ought to deliberately check those before running them. You'll have to run those contents as an advantaged client, and in the event that they contain malware, you could be giving over full control of your framework.

It's a superior plan to keep away from the circumstance by getting into the propensity for utilizing the - v choice and utilizing the volume compartment

Docker makes volumes in another manner that we haven't talked about. Picture metadata can give volume determinations In these cases, you may not know about the volumes made for new holders. This is simply the essential motivation to prepare to utilize the - v choice.

Vagrant volumes render plate space unusable until you've tidied them up. You can limit this issue by making sure to tidy them up and utilizing a volume compartment design.

CLEANUP Before perusing further, take a couple of seconds to tidy up the containers that you've made. Use docker ps - a to get a rundown of those holders and make sure to utilize the - v banner on docker rm to forestall vagrant volumes.

Coming up next is a solid case of expelling a compartment from one of the previous models:

docker rm - v understudy

Then again, in case you're utilizing a POSIX-agreeable shell, you can expel every halted holder and their volumes with the accompanying command:

docker rm - v $(docker ps - aq)

Anyway, you achieve the assignment, tidying up volumes is a significant piece of asset the board. Since you have a firm handle on the volume life cycle, sharing mechanisms, and use cases, you ought to be prepared to find out about cutting edge volume designs.

Propelled container designs with volumes

In reality, volumes are used to achieve a wide scope of record framework customizations and container collaborations. This segment centers around two or three progressed yet regular examples that you may experience or have the motivation to utilize in your very own frameworks.

Volume container design

I utilized an example called a volume container, which is a container that does minimal more than giving a handle to volumes. This is valuable on the off chance that you run over a case for offering a lot of volumes to numerous containers, or on the off chance that you can order a lot of volumes that fit a typical use case;

A volume container shouldn't run in light of the fact that halted containers keep up their volume references. A few of the models you've perused so far utilized the volume container design. The model containers cassshared, fowler, knuth, chomsky, and lamport all ran a straightforward reverberation direction to print something to the terminal and afterward left. At that point you utilized the halted containers as hotspots for the - volumes-from banner when making shopper containers.

Volume containers are significant for keeping an idea about data even in situations where a solitary container should have selective access to certain data. These handles cause it conceivable to effortlessly back up, to reestablish, and move data.

Assume you needed to refresh your database programming (utilize another picture). On the off chance that your database container composes its state to a volume and that volume was characterized by a vol-ume container, the relocation would be as basic as closing down the first data-base container and beginning the enhanced one with the volume container as a volume source. Reinforcement and reestablish tasks could be dealt with correspondingly. This, obviously, expect the new database programming can peruse the capacity organization of the old programming, and it searches for the data at a similar area.

TIP Using a container name prefix, for example, vc_ would be an incredible clue for people or contents not to utilize the - v choice when erasing a container. The particular prefix isn't as significant as setting up some show that peo-ple in your group and the instruments you assemble can depend on.

Volume containers are most valuable when you control and can institutionalize on mount point naming shows. This is on the grounds that each container that duplicates volumes from a volume container acquires its mount point definitions. For instance, a volume container that characterizes a volume mounted at/logs may be helpful to other contain-ers that hope to have the option to get to a volume mounted at/logs. Along these lines, a volume and its mount point become a kind of agreement between containers. Hence, pictures that have explicit volume necessities ought to impart those in their documentation or figure out how to do so automatically.

A model where two containers differ may be the place a volume container contributes a volume mounted at/logs, however, the container that utilizations - volumes-from is hoping to discover logs at/var/logs. For this situation, the devouring container would be not able to access the material it needs, and the framework would come up short.

Consider another model with a volume container named vc_data that contrib-utes two volumes:/data and/application. A container that has a reliance on the/data volume gave by vc_data yet utilizes/application for something different would break if both vol-umes were replicated along these lines. These two containers are contrary. However Docker has no chance to get of deciding purpose. The blunder wouldn't be found until after the new container was made and bombed somehow or another.

The volume container design is more about effortlessness and show than everything else. It's a basic device for working with data in Docker and can be stretched out in a couple of intriguing ways.

Data-stuffed volume containers

You can expand the volume container example and worth included by pressing containers with data, Once you've adjusted your containers to utilize volumes, you'll discover a wide range of events to share volumes. Volume containers are in a novel situation to seed volumes with data. The data-pressed volume container augmentation formalizes that thought. It depicts how pictures can be utilized to appropriate static assets like design or code for use in containers made with different pictures.

A data-stuffed volume container is worked from a picture that duplicates static content from its picture to volumes it characterizes. In doing as such, these containers can be utilized to appropriate basic engineering data like setup, key material, and code.

You can construct these by hand in the event that you have a picture that has the data you'd like to make accessible by running and characterizing the volume and running a cp direction at container-creation time:

```
docker run --name dpvc \
-v/config \
dockerinaction/ch4_packed /bin/sh -c 'cp /packed/* /config/'
docker run --rm --volumes-from dpvc \
alpine:latest ls /config
docker run --rm --volumes-from dpvc \
alpine:latest cat /config/packedData
docker rm -v dpvc
```

The commands in this code share files distributed by a single image. You created three containers: one data-packed volume container and two that copied its volume and inspected the contents of the volume. Again, this is a toy example, but it demonstrates the way that you might consider distributing configuration in your own situations. Using data-packed volume containers to inject material into a new container is the basis for the polymorphic container pattern discussed in the next section.

Polymorphic container pattern

As I stated earlier in the chapter, a polymorphic tool is one that you interact with in a consistent way but might have several implementations that do different things. Using volumes, you can inject different behavior into containers without modifying an image. A polymorphic container is one that provides some functionality that's easily substituted using volumes. For example, you may have an image that contains the binaries for Node.JS and by default executes a command that runs the Node.JS pro-gram located at /app/app.js. The image might contain some default implementation that simply prints "This is a Node.JS application" to the terminal.

You can change the behavior of containers created from this image by injecting your own app.js implementation using a volume mounted at /app/app.js. It might make more sense to layer that new functionality in a new image, but there are some cases when this is the best solution. The first is during development when you might not want to build a new image each time you iterate. The second is during operational events.

Consider a situation where an operational issue has occurred. In order to triage the issue, you might need tools available in an image that you had not anticipated when the image was built. But if you mount a volume where you make additional tools available, you can use the docker exec command to run additional processes in a container:

```
docker run --name tools dockerinaction/ch4_tools
docker run --rm \
--volumes-from tools \
alpine:latest \
ls /operations/*

docker run -d --name important_application \

--volumes-from tools \

dockerinaction/ch4_ia

docker exec important_application /operations/tools/someTool

docker rm -vf important_application

docker rm -v tools
```

You can infuse documents into generally static containers to change a wide range of conduct. Most ordinarily, you'll use polymorphic containers to infuse application design. Consider a multi-state arrangement pipeline where an application's setup would change contingent upon where you convey it. You may utilize data-pressed volume containers to contribute condition explicit arrangement at each stage, and afterward your application would search for its setup at some known area:

```
docker run --name devConfig \
-v /config \
dockerinaction/ch4_packed_config:latest \
/bin/sh -c 'cp /development/* /config/'
docker run --name prodConfig \
-v /config \
dockerinaction/ch4_packed_config:latest \
/bin/sh -c 'cp /production/* /config/'
docker run --name devApp \
--volumes-from devConfig \
dockerinaction/ch4_polyapp
docker run --name prodApp \
--volumes-from prodConfig \
dockerinaction/ch4_polyapp
```

You can infuse records into generally static containers to change a wide range of conduct. Most ordinarily, you'll use polymorphic containers to infuse application arrangement. Consider a multi-state arrangement pipeline where an application's setup would change contingent upon where you convey it. You may utilize data-pressed volume containers to contribute condition explicit arrangement at each stage, and afterward your application would search for its setup at some known area:

In this model, you start a similar application twice yet with an alternate design document infused. Utilizing this example you can assemble a straightforward variant controlled design conveyance framework.

Summary

One of the primary significant obstacles in figuring out how to utilize Docker is getting volumes and the document framework. This section covers volumes top to bottom, including the accompanying:

■ Volumes enable containers to impart documents to the host or different containers.

■ Volumes are portions of the host record framework that Docker mounts into containers at indicated areas.

■ There are two kinds of volumes: Docker-oversaw volumes that are situated in the Docker part of the host document framework and tie mount volumes that are found anyplace on the host record framework.

■ Volumes have life cycles that are autonomous of a particular container, yet a client can just reference Docker-oversaw volumes with a container handle.

■ The vagrant volume issue can make plate space hard to recoup. Utilize the - v alternative on docker rm to dodge the issue.

■ The volume container design is helpful for keeping your volumes sorted out and evading the vagrant volume issue.

■ The data-pressed volume container design is valuable for disseminating static substance for different containers.

■ The polymorphic container design is an approach to form insignificant practical segments and augment reuse.

Network exposure

In the past part you read about how to utilize volumes and work with documents in a compartment. This section manages another regular type of info and yield: network get to.

On the off chance that you have to run a site, database, email server, or any product that relies upon networking, similar to an internet browser inside a Docker compartment, at that point you have to understand how to connect that holder to the network. In the wake of perusing this part you'll have the option to make compartments with network presentation fitting for the application you're running, use network programming in one holder from another, and understand how compartments cooperate with the host and the host's network.

Networking foundation

A brisk diagram of pertinent networking ideas will be useful for understanding the points in this section. This area incorporates just elevated level detail; so in case you're a specialist, don't hesitate to skirt ahead.

Networking is tied in with imparting between forms that could conceivably have a similar nearby assets. To know the material in this section you just need to consider a couple of essential network reflections that are generally utilized by forms. The better understanding you have of networking, the more you'll find out about the mechanics at work. Be that as it may, a profound understanding isn't required to utilize the instruments gave by Docker. On the off chance that anything, the material contained in this should provoke you to freely look into chosen ridiculously up. Those essential deliberations utilized by forms incorporate protocols, network interfaces, and ports.

Basics: protocols, interfaces, and ports

A convention concerning correspondence and networking is a kind of language. Two parties that concur on a convention can understand what each other is conveying. This is vital to successful correspondence. Hypertext Transfer Protocol (HTTP) is one famous network convention that numerous individuals have known about. The convention professional vides the World Wide Web. Countless network protocols and a few layers of correspondence are made by those protocols. For the present, it's just significant that you comprehend what a convention is so you can understand network interfaces and ports.

A network interface has a location and speaks to an area. You can consider between faces as undifferentiated from true areas with addresses. A network interface resembles a letter drop. Messages are conveyed to a letter drop for beneficiaries at that address, and mes-sages are taken from a post box to be conveyed somewhere else.

While a letter box has a postal location, a network interface has an IP address, which is characterized by the Internet Protocol. The subtleties of IP are intriguing however outside of the extent of this book. The significant thing to think about IP addresses is that they are one of a kind in their network and contain data about their area on their network.

It's normal for PCs to have two sorts of interfaces: an Ethernet interface and a loopback interface. An Ethernet interface is what you're likely generally acquainted with. It's utilized to connect to different interfaces and procedures. A loopback interface isn't connected to some other interface. From the outset this may appear to be futile, however it's frequently valuable to have the option to utilize network protocols to speak with different projects on a similar PC. In those cases a loopback is an extraordinary arrangement.

With regards to the post box allegory, a port resembles a beneficiary or a sender. There may be a few people who get messages at a solitary location. For instance, a solitary location may get messages for Wendy Webserver, Deborah

As a general rule, ports are simply numbers and characterized as a major aspect of the Transmission Control Protocol (TCP). Again the subtleties of the convention are past the extent of this book, however I urge you to find out about it some time. Individuals who made standards for star tocols, or organizations that claim a specific item, choose what port number ought to be utilized for explicit purposes. For instance, web servers give HTTP on port 80 as a matter of course. MySQL, a database item, serves its convention on port 3306 of course. Memcached, a quick reserve innovation, gives its convention on port 11211. Ports are composed on TCP messages simply like names are composed on envelopes.

Interfaces, protocols, and ports are on the whole quick worries for programming and clients. By finding out about these things, you build up a superior gratefulness for the manner in which genius grams impart and how your PC fits into the master plan.

Greater picture: networks, NAT, and port sending

Interfaces are single focuses in bigger networks. Networks are characterized in the manner that interfaces are connected together, and that linkage decides an interface's IP address.

Here and there a message has a beneficiary that an interface isn't legitimately connected to, so all things considered it's conveyed to a middle person that realizes how to course the message for conveyance. Returning to the mail illustration, this is like how certifiable mail vehicle riers work.

At the point when you place a message in your outbox, a mail transporter lifts it up and conveys it to a nearby steering office. That office is itself an interface. It will take the message and send it along to the following stop on the course to a goal. A neighborhood steering office for a mail bearer may advance a message to a local office, and then to a nearby office for the goal, and at last to the beneficiary. It's normal for network courses to pursue a comparable example.

This section is worried about interfaces that exist on a solitary PC, so the networks and courses we consider won't be anyplace close to that muddled. Actually, this section is around two explicit networks and the manner in which compartments are appended to them. The main network is the one that your PC is connected to. The second one is a virtual network that Docker makes to connect the entirety of the running compartments to the network that the PC is connected to. That subsequent network is known as a scaffold.

Similarly as the name suggests, an extension is an interface that connects numerous networks with the goal that they can work as a solitary network, Bridges work by specifically sending traffic between the connected networks dependent on another kind of network address. To know the material in this section, you just should be OK with this unique thought.

This has been an extremely harsh prologue to some nuanced subjects. I've extremely just started to expose what's underneath so as to assist you with understanding how to utilize Docker and the networking offices that it rearranges.

Docker container networking

Docker is worried about two kinds of networking: single-have virtual networks and multi-have networks. Neighborhood virtual networks are utilized to give container separation. Multi-have virtual networks give an overlay where any container on a taking an interest host can have its very own routable IP address from some other container in the network.

This part covers single-have virtual networks inside and out. Understanding how Docker separates containers on the network is basic for the security-disapproved. Individuals building networked applications need to know how containerization will affect their arrangement necessities.

Multi-have networking is still in beta at the hour of this composition. Executing it requires a more extensive understanding of other biological system instruments notwithstanding understand-ing the material covering single-have networking. Until multi-have networking settles, it's ideal to begin by understanding how Docker assembles neighborhood virtual networks.

The neighborhood Docker network topology

Docker utilizes highlights of the hidden working framework to manufacture a particular and adaptable virtual network topology. The virtual network is neighborhood to the machine where Docker is introduced and is comprised of courses between taking an interest containers and the more extensive network where the host is connected. You can change the conduct of that network structure and now and again change the structure itself by utilizing command-line alternatives for beginning the Docker daemon and every container.

Containers have their private interface and a different Ethernet interface connected to another virtual interface in the host's namespace. These two connected interfaces structure a connection between the host's network stack and the stack made for every container. Much the same as common home networks, every container is appointed a remarkable private IP address that is not straightforwardly reachable from the outer network. Connections are directed through the Docker connect interface called docker0. You can think about the docker0 interface like your home switch. Every one of the virtual interfaces made for containers is connected to docker0, and together they structure a network. This scaffold between face is connected to the network where the host is appended.

Utilizing the docker command-line apparatus, you can redo the IP tends to utilized, the host interface that docker0 is connected to, and the manner in which containers speak with one another. The connections between interfaces depict how uncovered or separated a particular network container is from the remainder of the network. Docker utilizes bit namespaces to make those private virtual interfaces, yet the namespace itself doesn't give the network disengagement. Network introduction or seclusion is given by the host's firewall governs (each advanced Linux appropriation runs a firewall). With the choices gave, there are four models for network containers.

Four network container prime examples

All Docker containers tail one of four prime examples. These prime examples characterize how a container communicates with other neighborhood containers and the host's network. Every fill an alternate need, and you can think about each as having an alternate level of disengagement. At the point when you use Docker to make a container, it's imperative to deliberately think about what you need to achieve and utilize the most grounded conceivable container without trading off that objective.

The four are prime examples are these:

■Closed containers

■Joined containers

■Bridged containers

■Open containers

Throughout the following four subsections I present every model. Not many perusers will have an event to utilize every one of the four. In finding out about how to fabricate them and when to utilize them, you'll have the option to make that differentiation yourself.

Shut containers

The most grounded sort of network container is one that doesn't permit any network traffic. These are called shut containers. Procedures running in such a container will approach just to a loopback interface. In the event that they have to discuss just with themselves or one another, this will be reasonable. In any case, any program that expects access to the network or the web won't work accurately in such a container. For instance, if the product needs to download refreshes, it won't have the option to in light of the fact that it can't utilize the network.

Most perusers will originate from a server programming or web application background, and in that setting it very well may be hard to envision a down to earth use for a con-tainer that has no network get to. There are many number of approaches to utilize Docker that it's anything but difficult to disregard volume containers, reinforcement employments, disconnected cluster preparing, or diagnos-tic apparatuses. The test you face isn't advocating Docker for each element yet realizing which highlights best fit the utilization cases that you may be underestimating.

Docker fabricates this sort of container by just avoiding the progression where an exter-nally available network interface is made, the shut prime example has no connection to the Docker connect interface. Projects in these con-tainers can talk just to themselves.

All Docker containers, including shut containers, approach a private interface. You may have experiences with loopback interfaces as of now. It's regular for individuals with moderate understanding to have utilized localhost or 127.0.0.1 as a location in a URL. In these cases you were advising a program to tie to or contact a help bound to your PC's loopback network interface.

By making private loopback interfaces for every container, Docker empowers star grams run inside a container to impart through the network however without that correspondence leaving the container.

You can advise Docker to make a shut container by determining none with the - net banner as a contention to the docker run command:

docker run --rm \

--net none \

alpine:latest \

ip addr

By running this example, you can see that the only available network interface is the return interface, linked to 127.0.0.1. This configuration means three things:

■ Any program running in the container can connect to or wait for connections on this interface.

■ Nothing outside the container can be associated with this interface.

■ No programs running inside this container can reach anything outside the container.

This last point is important and easily demonstrable. If you are connected to the Internet, try to communicate with a popular service that should always be available. In this case, try communicating with Google's public DNS service:

```
docker run --rm \
--net no \
Alpine: last \
ping -w 2 8.8.8.8
```

In this example, create a closed container and try to test the speed between your container and the public DNS server provided by Google. This attempt should succeed with a message such as "ping: send to: network unavailable". This makes sense because we know that the container does not have a path to a larger network.

When to use sealed containers

Closed containers shall be used when there is a need for network isolation or the program does not require network access. For example, running a text editor on a terminal does not require network access. Running a random password generation program must be done inside a container without network access to prevent this number from being stolen.

There are not many ways to customize the network configuration for a closed container. Although this species may seem too restrictive, it is the safest of the four options and can be expanded to make it more comfortable. These are not the default values for Docker containers, but it is recommended that you try to justify the use of any weaker element before doing so. Docker creates default containers for the bridge.

Bridged containers

Bridge containers facilitate network isolation and therefore make it easier to start. This archetype is the most adaptable and should be strengthened as a recommended practice. Bridge containers have a private loopback interface and another private interface connected to the rest of the computer via a network bridge.

This section is the longest in this chapter. Bridge containers are the most common archetype of network containers. This chapter introduces several new options that you can use with other archetypes.

All interfaces associated with docker0 are part of the same virtual subnet. This means that they can talk to each other and communicate with a larger network through the docker0 interface.

Reach out

The most common reason for choosing a bridged container is because the process must have access to the network. You can skip --net to create a bridge container the ability to execute a command from a fixed menu or you can set its value in the bridge. I use each shape in the following examples:

```
docker run --rm \
- network bridge \
Alpine: last \
ip address
```

Like the first example for closed containers, this command will create a new container from the last Alpine image and list the available network interfaces. This time, two interfaces will be displayed: Ethernet interface and local loop. The output will include details such as IP address and subnet mask of each interface, maximum packet size (MTU), and various interface metrics.

Now that you have confirmed that your mailbox has a different interface with an IP address, try accessing the network again. This time skip the --net flag to see that the bridge is the default Docker network container type:

```
docker run --rm \
Alpine: last \
ping -w 2 8.8.8.8
```

Pinging a public DNS server from Google from this bridge container works and no additional features are needed. After executing this command, your container will ping for two seconds and generate a report of the network statistics collected.

You now know that if you have software that needs to access the Internet or another PC on a private network, you can also use a bridged container.

CNR

Domain Name System is a protocol for assigning host names to IP addresses. This task allows clients to group dependencies on a specific host IP address and depend on a host specified by a known name. The most basic way to change outbound communication is to create a name for the IP addresses.

Containers in bridge networks and other computers in your network usually have IP addresses that cannot be routed publicly. This means that if you do not use your own DNS server, you cannot name it. Docker offers several options for customizing the DNS settings of a new container.

First, the docker start command has a --hostime flag that you can use to set the hostname of the new container. This indicator adds an entry to the DNS replacement system inside the container. The entry assigns the host name given to the IP address of the tank bridge:

```
docker run --rm \
- Hostname \
Alpine: last \
Nslookup bark
```

This example creates a new container named barker host and runs a program to find the IP address of the same name. Running this example will generate an output similar to this:

```
Server: 10.0.2.3
Address 1: 10.0.2.3
Name: bark
Address 1: 172.17.0.22 Barker
```

The IP address in the last line is the bridge IP address for the new container. The IP address listed on the line named Server is the address of the server that gave the task.

The container hostname definition is useful when programs running inside the container need to search for their own IP address or just identify themselves. As other containers do not know this computer name, their use is limited. If you use an external DNS, you can share these host names.

Another option for customizing the DNS configuration of the mailbox is the ability to specify one or more DNS servers to use. To illustrate this, the following example creates a new mailbox and configures a DNS server for this mailbox in Google's public DNS service:

```
docker run --rm \
--dns 8.8.8.8 \
Alpine: last \
nslookup docker.com
```

Using a specific DNS can provide consistency if you use Docker on a laptop, and it often moves between ISPs. It is a key tool for people creating services and networks. Here are some important notes about setting up your own DNS:

■ The value must be an IP. If you think about that, the reason is obvious. The container would need a DNS server to look up the name.

■ The --dns = [] flag can be configured several times to define several DNS servers (in case one or more of them are not available).

■ The --dns = [] flag can be set when you launch the Docker daemon by running in the background. When you do, these DNS servers will default to each mailbox. But if you close the daemon when the mailboxes start and change the default values when restarting, the current mailboxes will retain their previous DNS settings. You must restart these containers for the change to take effect.

The third option related to DNS, --dns-search = [], allows you to specify a DNS search domain that looks like the default hostname suffix. The game will search for any host names that do not have a known top-level domain (such as .com or .net) with the given suffix.

```
docker run --rm \
--dns-search docker.com \
occupied: last \
nslookup Registry.hub
```

This command will resolve the IP address of register.hub.docker.com because the DNS lookup domain provided will complete the hostname.

This feature is most commonly used for trivial reasons, such as the name of direct access to internal corporate networks. For example, your company may manage an internal documentation wiki that you can easily refer to at http: // wiki /. But it can also be much more powerful.

Suppose you maintain a single DNS for your development and test environment. Instead of creating environmentally compatible software (with environment-specific coded names, such as myservice.dev.mycompany.com), you might want to consider using non-environmentally sensitive search names and DNS names (such as myservice):

```
docker run --rm \
--dns-search dev.mycompany \
occupied: last \
nslookup myservice
docker run --rm \
--dns-search test.mycompany \
occupied: last \
nslookup myservice
```

With this model, the only change is the context in which the program is running. As with custom DNS servers, you can provide multiple custom search domains for the same mailbox. Simply flag the number of times you have a search domain.

For example:

```
docker run --rm \
--dns-search my company \
--dns-search myothercompany ...
```

This indicator can also be set when you launch the Docker daemon to set defaults for each container created. Again, remember that these options are set for the container only when created. If you change the default values while the tank is running, the tank will retain the previous values.

The last DNS feature to consider is the ability to replace DNS. This system uses the same system as the --hostname flag. The --add-host = [] flag of the runtime command in the fixed menu allows you to specify a custom task for the IP address and pair of host names:

```
docker run --rm \
--Add host test: 10.10.10.255 \
Alpine: last \
nslookup test
```

Like --dns and --dns-search, the option can be specified several times. But unlike other options, this indicator cannot be set by default when the daemon is launched.

This feature is a type of name resolution scalpel. Providing specific name assignments for individual containers is the best possible customization. You can use them to effectively block the destination host name by assigning them a known IP address, such as 127.0.0.1. You can use it to route traffic to a specific destination via a proxy. This is often used to route insecure traffic through secure channels, such as the SSH tunnel. Adding these replacements is a trick that web developers have been using for years to use their own local copies of the web application. If you spend some time thinking about the interface that assigns a name to an IP address, I'm sure you can offer all kinds of uses.

All custom tasks are in a file located in / etc / hosts in its container. If you want to see what substitutions exist, all you have to do is review that file. The rules for editing and analyzing this file are available online

```
docker run --rm \
- mycontainer name \
--add-host docker.com:127.0.0.1 \
--add-host test: 10.10.10.2 \ alpine: last \ cat / etc / hosts
```

This should have a result similar to this:

```
172.17.0.45 mycontainer
127.0.0.1 localhost
:: 1 localhost ip6-localhost ip6-loopback
fe00 :: 0 ip6-localnet
ff00 :: 0 ip6-mcastprefix
ff02 :: 1 ip6-allnodes
ff02 :: 2 ip6-allrouters
Test 10.10.10.2
127.0.0.1 docker.com
```

DNS is a powerful behavior change system. The name map / IP address provides a simple interface that users and programs can use to separate them from specific network addresses. If DNS is the best tool for changing outbound traffic behavior, a firewall and network topology are your best tools for controlling inbound traffic.

Opening inbound communication

Bridged containers aren't open from the host organize of course. Containers are ensured by your host's firewall framework. The default arrange topology gives no course from the host's outer interface to a container interface. That implies there's simply no real way to get to a container from outside the host.

Containers wouldn't be extremely valuable if there were no real way to get to them through the system. Fortunately, that is not the situation. The docker run order gives a banner, - p=[] or - publish=[], that you can use to make a mapping between a port on the host's system stack and the new container's interface. You've utilized this a couple of times prior in this book, however it merits referencing once more. The arrangement of the mapping can have four structures:

- <containerPort>

This structure ties the container port to a powerful port on the entirety of the host's between faces:

docker run - p 3333 ...

- <hostPort>:<containerPort>

This structure ties the predefined container port to the predetermined port on every one of the host's interfaces:

docker run - p 3333:3333 ...

- <ip>::<containerPort>

This structure ties the container port to a unique port on the interface with the predefined IP address:

docker run - p 192.168.0.32::2222 ...

- <ip>:<hostPort>:<containerPort>

This structure ties the container port to the predetermined port on the interface with the predefined IP address:

```
docker run - p 192.168.0.32:1111:1111 ...
```

These models expect that your host's IP address is 192.168.0.32. This is self-assertive however valuable to exhibit the component. Every one of the direction sections will make a course from a port on a host interface to a particular port on the container's interface. The various structures offer a scope of granularity and control. This banner is another that can be rehashed the same number of times as you have to give the ideal arrangement of mappings.

The docker run direction gives a substitute method to achieve opening channels. In the event that you can acknowledge a dynamic or vaporous port task on the host, you can utilize the - P, or - distribute all, banner. This banner advises the Docker daemon to make mappings, similar to the primary type of the - p choice for all ports that a picture reports, to expose. Pictures convey a rundown of ports that are exposed for straightforwardness and as an insight to clients where contained administrations are tuning in. For instance, on the chance that you realize that a picture like dockerinaction/ch5_expose exposes ports 5000, 6000, and 7000, every one of the accompanying directions accomplish something very similar:

```
docker run - d - name dawson \
- p 5000 \
- p 6000 \
- p 7000 \
dockerinaction/ch5_expose
docker run - d - name woolery \
- P \
dockerinaction/ch5_expose
```

It's anything but difficult to perceive how this can spare a client some composing, yet it asks two inquiries. To begin with, how is this utilized if the picture doesn't expose the port you need to utilize? Second, how would you find which dynamic ports were doled out?

The docker run order gives another banner, - expose, that takes a port number that the container should expose. This banner can be set on different occasions, once for each port:

```
docker run - d - name philbin \
- expose 8000 \
- P \
dockerinaction/ch5_expose
```

Utilizing - expose along these lines will add port 8000 to the rundown of ports that ought to be bound to dynamic ports utilizing the - P banner. In the wake of running the model, you can perceive what these ports were mapped to by utilizing docker ps, docker investigate, or another direction, docker port. The port sub-command takes either the container name or ID as a contention and produces a straightforward rundown with one port guide section for each line:

docker port philbin

Running this direction should create a rundown like the accompanying:

5000/tcp - > 0.0.0.0:49164

6000/tcp - > 0.0.0.0:49165

7000/tcp - > 0.0.0.0:49166

8000/tcp - > 0.0.0.0:49163

With the instruments canvassed in this segment, you ought to have the option to oversee directing any inbound traffic to the right bridged container running on your host. There's one other unpretentious sort of communication: between container communication.

Intercontainer communication

As an update, every one of the containers secured so far utilize the Docker bridge system to speak with one another and the system that the host is on. All neighborhood bridged containers are on a similar bridge arrange and can speak with one another as a matter of course.

So as to ensure that you have a full thankfulness for this transparency, the following order shows how containers can impart over this system:

```
docker run - it - rm dockerinaction/ch5_nmap - sS - p 3333 172.17.0.0/24
```

This direction will run a program called nmap to check every one of the interfaces connected to the bridge arrange. For this situation it's searching for any interface that is tolerating associations on port 3333. On the off chance that you had such an assistance running in another container, this direction would have found it, and you could utilize another program to associate with it.

Permitting communication along these lines makes it easy to assemble participating containers. No extra work should be done to construct pipes between containers. It's as free as an open system. This might be middle of the road however can be hazardous for clients who are uninformed. It's normal for programming to dispatch with low-security highlights like default pass-words or debilitated encryption. Guileless clients may anticipate that the system topology or some neighborhood firewall will shield containers from open get to. This is consistent with some degree, yet as a matter of course any container is completely available from some other neighborhood container.

At the point when you start the Docker daemon, you can arrange it to refuse organize associations between containers. Doing so is a best practice in multi-occupant conditions. It limits the focuses (called an assault surface) where an assailant may bargain other containers. You can accomplish this by setting - icc=false when you start the Docker daemon:

```
docker - d - icc=false ...
```

When between container communication is handicapped, any traffic starting with one container then onto the next will be obstructed by the host's firewall aside from where unequivocally permitted.

Debilitating between container communications is an important advance in any Docker-empowered condition. In doing as such, you make a situation where express conditions must be announced so as to work appropriately. Best case scenario, an increasingly unbridled setup enables containers to be begun when their conditions aren't prepared. Even from a pessimistic standpoint, leaving between container communication empowered permits traded off projects inside containers to assault other neighborhood containers.

Modifying the bridge interface

Before proceeding onward to the following paradigm, this appears to be a fitting time to show the design choices that change the bridge interface. Outside this segment, models will consistently expect that you're working with the default bridge design.

Docker gives three choices to tweaking the bridge interface that the Docker daemon expands on first startup. These choices let the client do the accompanying:

■ Define the location and subnet of the bridge

■ Define the scope of IP tends to that can be appointed to containers

■ Define the most extreme transmission unit (MTU)

To define the Internet Prootocol address of the bridge and the subnet go, utilize the - bip banner when you start the Docker daemon. There's a wide range of reasons why you should utilize a different IP run for your bridge arrange. At the point when you experience one of those circumstances, making the change is as basic as using one banner.

Using the - bip banner (which stands for bridge IP), you can set the IP address of the bridge interface that Docker will create and the size of the subnet using a tactless inter-domain routing (CIDR) arranged location. CIDR notation gives an approach to determine an IP address and its routing prefix. See informative supplement B for a short introduction on CIDR notation. There are a few aides online detailing how to construct CIDR arranged locations; however in case you're acquainted with bit masking, the following model will be adequate to kick you off.

Assume you need to set your bridge IP address to 192.168.0.128 and assign the last 128 locations in that subnet prefix to the bridge arrange. All things considered, you'd set the estimation of - bip to 192.168.0.128/25. To be unequivocal, using this worth will create the docker0 interface, set its IP address to 192.168.0.128, and permit IP tends to that range from 192.168.0.128 to 192.168.0.255. The command would be like this:

docker - d - bip "192.168.0.128" ...

With a system defined for the bridge, you can proceed to redo which IP addresses in that system can be doled out to new containers. To do as such, give a comparative CIDR notation portrayal to the - fixed-cidr banner.

Working from the past circumstance, if you needed to hold just the last 64 locations of the system doled out to the bridge interface, you would utilize 192.168.0.192/26. At the point when the Docker daemon is begun with this set, new containers will get an IP address somewhere in the range of 192.168.0.192 and 192.168.0.255. The main admonition with this alternative is that the range determined must be a subnet of the system doled out to the bridge (in case you're confounded, there's bunches of extraordinary documentation and tooling on the internet to help):

docker - d - fixed-cidr "192.168.0.192/26"

I'm not going to spend an excessive amount of exertion on the last setting. System interfaces have a breaking point to the greatest size of a bundle (a parcel is a nuclear unit of correspondence). By convention, Ethernet interfaces have a most extreme bundle size of 1500 bytes. This is the arranged default. In some particular instances, you'll have to change the MTU on the Docker bridge. At the point when you experience such a situation, you can utilize the - mtu banner to set the size in bytes:

```
docker - d – mtu 1200
```

Clients who are increasingly OK with Linux networking natives may jump at the chance to realize that they can give their very own custom bridge interface instead of using the default bridge. To do as such, design your bridge interface and then advise the Docker daemon to utilize it instead of docker0 when you start the daemon. The banner to utilize is - b or - bridge.

On the off chance that you've arranged a bridge named mybridge, you'd start Docker with a command like the following:

```
docker - d - b mybridge ...
docker - d - bridge mybridge ...
```

Building custom bridges requires a more profound understanding of Linux portion instruments than is important for this book. However, you should realize that this capacity is accessible on the off chance that you do the examination required.

Joined containers

The following less separated system container model is known as a joined container. These containers share a typical system stack. In this manner, there's no confinement between joined containers. This implies decreased control and security. In spite of the fact that this isn't the least secure paradigm, it's where the dividers of prison have been torn down.

Docker fabricates this sort of a container by providing access to the interfaces created for a particular container to another new container. Interfaces are in this manner shared like oversaw volumes.

The simplest method to see joined containers in activity is to utilize an uncommon case and join it with another container. The main command begins a server that tunes in on the loopback interface. The subsequent command records all the open ports. The subsequent command records the open port created by the main command in light of the fact that the two containers share a similar system interface:

```
docker run - d - name brady \
```

```
- net none alpine: latest \
nc - l 127.0.0.1:3333
docker run - it \
- net container:brady \
alpine: latest netstat – al
```

By running these commands you can create two containers that offer a similar network interface. Since the main container is created as a shut container, the two will just share that single loopback interface. The container estimation of the - net banner gives you a chance to indicate the container that the new container ought to be joined with. Either the container name or its crude ID recognizes the container that the new container ought to reuse.

Containers joined in this manner will maintain different types of detachment. They will keep different file systems, different memory, and so on. Be that as it may, they will have precisely the same system parts. That may sound concerning, however this sort of container can be helpful.

In the last model, you joined two containers on a system interface that has no entrance to the bigger system. In doing in this way, you expanded the handiness of a shut container. You may utilize this example when two different projects with access to two different bits of information need to communicate yet shouldn't share direct access to different's information. Then again, you may utilize this example when you have arranged administrations that need to communicate yet organise access or administration disclosure systems like DNS are inaccessible.

Setting aside security concerns, using joined containers reintroduces port clash issues. A client ought to know about this at whatever point they're joining two containers. It's feasible on the off chance that they're joining containers that run comparable administrations that they will create conflicts. Under those conditions, the conflicts should be settled using progressively conventional techniques like changing application design. These conflicts can happen on any common interfaces. At the point when projects are run outside a container, they share access to the host's interfaces with each other program running on the PC, so this particular degree increase is as yet an enhancement for the present business as usual.

At the point when two containers are joined, all interfaces are shared, and conflicts may hap-pen on any of them. From the outset, it may appear to be senseless to join two containers that need bridge get to. All things considered, they would already be able to communicate over the Docker bridge subnet. Be that as it may, consider circumstances where one procedure needs to screen the other through generally ensured channels. Correspondence between containers is dependent upon firewall rules. In the event that one procedure needs to communicate with another on an unexposed port, the best thing to do might be to join the containers.

Use associated containers when you want to use a single communication interface to communicate between programs in different containers.

Use the provided containers if the program in the container must modify the associated network string and another program uses that modified network.

Use associated mailboxes when you need to monitor network traffic from one application to another mailbox.

Before you start talking about Docker insecurity, since it allows any new container to join the current container, please note that privileged access is required to issue Docker commands. Privileged attackers can do whatever they want, including directly attacking code or data that is executed in any container. In this context, this type of network beam manipulation is not serious.

The big problem is in contexts where people build multi-tenant systems. If you create or plan to use this service, first set up a few accounts and try to access each other. If you can, think twice before using the service for something important. Joining another user's network bundle or mounting a volume is a wonderful problem.

The enclosed containers are a bit weaker, but they are not the weakest type of network containers. This title belongs to open containers.

Open containers

Open containers are dangerous. They do not have a network container and have full access to the host network. This includes access to host critical services. Open containers contain absolutely no insulation and should only be considered when you have no other options. The only useful quality is that non-privileged containers still cannot reconfigure the network string.

This type of container occurs when you specify a host as the value of the --net option in the fixed menu runtime command:

```
docker run --rm \
--host \
alpine: last ip address
```

Performing this command will create a container from the last Alpine image and no prison network. When you run ip addr in this container, you can view all the network interfaces of the host. You should see several interfaces in the list, including the docker0 call. As you noticed, this example creates a container that performs a discrete task and then deletes it immediately.

With this configuration, processes can be connected to secure network ports whose number is less than 1024.

Now that you've learned the type of network containers you can create with Docker and how these containers interact with the network, you need to learn how to use network software in one container from another. You've seen containers use a gateway network to communicate, and you may have started thinking about how to fill a small system. If you consider that the bridge network assigns IP addresses to mailboxes dynamically at creation time, discovering local services can seem complicated.

One solution to the problem is to use a local DNS server and registration point when starting the mailbox. Another solution would be to write in your programs to search the local area network for IP addresses for listening on known ports. Both approaches manage a dynamic environment but require a non-trivial load and additional tools. These approaches will fail if arbitrary communication in the container is disabled. You can force all traffic back and forth through the host interface into known published ports. However, sometimes you may need privileged access to the network port. Docker provides another tool you have already seen dealing with this use case.

Introducing local service discovery links

When you create a container, you can associate it with another container. This destination container must be started when a new container is created. The reason

It's simple. Containers keep their IP address only while they are running. If arrested, they lose their rent.

Adding a link to a new container has three effects:

■ Environment variables will be created that describes the destination of the destination container.

■ The nickname of the connection will be added to the DNS replacement list of the new mailbox with the destination mailbox IP address.

■ More interestingly, if mailbox-mail communication is disabled, Docker will add special firewall rules to allow communication between connected mailboxes.

The first two connection features are great for discovering basic services, but the third allows users to strengthen their local container networks without sacrificing container-to-container communication.

Ports open to communication are those that are exposed in the destination container. Therefore, the -expose flag provides direct access to a specific type of port port mapping container when ICC is enabled. When ICC is disabled, --expose becomes a tool for defining firewall rules and explicitly declaring a container interface on a network. In the same context, connections become a more static dependency statement for the local enforcement service. Here's a simple example. These images do not really exist:

```
docker run -d --name importantData \
--expose 3306 \
dockerinaction/mysql_noauth \
service mysql_noauth start
docker run -d --name importantWebapp \
--link imporantData:db \
dockerinaction/ch5_web startapp.sh -db tcp://db:3306
docker run -d --name buggyProgram \
dockerinaction/ch5_buggy
```

Reading through this model, you can see that I've begun some stupidly designed MySQL server (a prevalent database server). The name suggests that the server has disabled any verification necessities and any individual who can associate with the server can get to the information. I at that point began a significant web application that necessities access to the information in the importantData container. I included a link from the importantWebapp con-tainer to the importantData container. Docker will add information to that new container that will portray how to interface with importantData. This way, when the web application opens a database association with tcp://db:3306, it will interface with the database. Ultimately, I began another container that is known to contain carriage code. It's running as a nonprivileged customer, yet an assailant might be able to inspect the bridge organize if the program is undermined.

In case I'm running with inter-container correspondence empowered, assailants could without much of a stretch take the information from the database in the importantData container. They would have the option to do a basic system output to distinguish the open port and then gain access by basically opening an association. Indeed, even an easygoing traffic onlooker may think this association suitable in light of the fact that no container conditions have been emphatically displayed.

On the off chance that I was running this model with inter-container correspondence crippled, an assailant would be not able to arrive at some other containers from the container running the undermined software.

This is a genuinely senseless model. Kindly don't think that basically disabling inter-container correspondence will ensure assets if those assets don't secure themselves. With suitably arranged software, solid system administers, and pronounced help conditions, you can construct systems that accomplish great resistance inside and out.

Link aliases

Links are single direction arrange conditions created when one container is created and indicates a link to another. As referenced already, the - link banner utilized for this pur-present takes a single contention. That contention is a guide from a container name or ID to a moniker. The assumed name can be anything as long as it's extraordinary in the extent of the container is created. Thus, if three containers named a, b, and c as of now exist and are running, at that point I could run the following:

docker run - link a:alias-a - link b:alias-b - link c:alias-c ...

In any case, in the event that I committed an error and relegated a few or all containers to a similar pseudonym, at that point that assumed a name would just contain association information for one of the different containers. For this situation, the firewall rules would even now be created however would be about pointless with-out that association information.

Link aliases create a more elevated level issue. Software running inside a container has to know the assumed name of the container or host it's connecting to so it can play out the query. Like host names, link aliases become an image that numerous gatherings must concur on for a system to work accurately. Link aliases work as an agreement.

An engineer may assemble their application to expect that a database will have an assumed name of "database" and consistently search for it at tcp://database:3306 on the grounds that a DNS supersede with that host name would exist. This normal host name approach would function as long as the individual or procedure building the container either create a link associated with a database or utilizations - add-host to create the host name. On the other hand, the application could generally search for association information from a domain variable named DATABASE_PORT. The earth variable methodology will work just when a link is created with that moniker.

The issue is that there are no reliance announcements or runtime reliance checks. It's simple for the individual building the container to do as such without providing the necessary linkage. Docker clients should either depend on documentation to communicate these conditions or include custom reliance checking and fizzle quick conduct on The ports that are opened for correspondence are those that have been uncovered by the objective container. So the - uncover banner gives an alternate way to only one particu-lar kind of container to have port mapping when ICC is empowered. At the point when ICC is crippled, - uncover turns into a device for defining firewall rules and straightforward presentation of a con-tainer's interface on the system. In a similar setting, links become an increasingly static declaration of nearby runtime administration conditions. Here's a basic model; these images don't exist:

Container startup. I suggest building the reliance checking code first. For instance, the following content is included in dockerinaction/ch5_ff to approve that a link named "database" has been set at startup:

```
#!/bin/sh
in the event that [ - z ${DATABASE_PORT+x} ]
at that point
reverberation, "Link assumed name 'database' was not set!"
exit
else
executive "$@"
fi
```

You can see this content at work by running the following:

```
docker run -d - name mydb - uncover 3306 \
alpine:latest nc - l 0.0.0.0:3306
docker run -it - rm \
dockerinaction/ch5_ff reverberation This "shouldn't" work.
docker run -it - rm \
- link mydb:wrongalias \
dockerinaction/ch5_ff reverberation Wrong.
docker run -it - rm \
- link mydb:database \
dockerinaction/ch5_ff reverberation It worked.
docker stop mydb && docker rm mydb
```

This model content depends on the environment modifications made by Docker when links are created. You'll find these extremely valuable when you start building your own images

Environment modifications

I've referenced that creating a link will add association information to another container. This association information is injected in the new container by adding environment factors and a host name mapping in the DNS abrogate system. We should begin with a guide to inspect the link modifications:

```
docker run -d - name mydb \
- uncover 2222 - expose 3333 - uncover 4444/udp \
alpine:latest nc - l 0.0.0.0:2222
docker run -it - rm \
- link mydb:database \
dockerinaction/ch5_ff env
docker stop mydb && docker rm mydb
```
This should yield a square of lines that include the following:
```
DATABASE_PORT=tcp://172.17.0.23:3333
DATABASE_PORT_3333_TCP=tcp://172.17.0.23:3333
```

```
DATABASE_PORT_2222_TCP=tcp://172.17.0.23:2222
DATABASE_PORT_4444_UDP=udp://172.17.0.23:4444
DATABASE_PORT_2222_TCP_PORT=2222
DATABASE_PORT_3333_TCP_PORT=3333
DATABASE_PORT_4444_UDP_PORT=4444
DATABASE_PORT_3333_TCP_ADDR=172.17.0.23
DATABASE_PORT_2222_TCP_ADDR=172.17.0.23
DATABASE_PORT_4444_UDP_ADDR=172.17.0.23
DATABASE_PORT_2222_TCP_PROTO=tcp
DATABASE_PORT_3333_TCP_PROTO=tcp
DATABASE_PORT_4444_UDP_PROTO=udp
DATABASE_NAME=/furious_lalande/database
```

These are an example of environment factors created for a link. Every one of the factors relating to a particular link will utilize the link moniker as a prefix. There will consistently be a single variable with the _NAME addition that includes the name of the present container, a cut, and the link assumed name. For each port uncovered by the linked container, there will be four individual environment factors with the uncovered port in the variable name. The pat-terns are as per the following:

■ <ALIAS>_PORT_<PORT NUMBER>_<PROTOCOL TCP or UDP>_PORT

This variable will essentially contain the port number. That is interested on the grounds that the worth will be contained in the variable name. This could be helpful in case you're filtering the rundown of environment factors for those containing the string TCP_PORT. Doing so would render the rundown of ports.

■ <ALIAS>_PORT_<PORT NUMBER>_<PROTOCOL TCP or UDP>_ADDR

The estimations of factors with this example will be the IP address of the container serving the association. In the event that the false name is the equivalent, these should all have a similar worth.

■ <ALIAS>_PORT_<PORT NUMBER>_<PROTOCOL TCP or UDP>_PROTO

Like factors with the _PORT postfix, the estimations of these factors are really contained within the variable name. It's significant not to expect that the convention will consistently be TCP. UDP is likewise bolstered.

■ <ALIAS>_PORT_<PORT NUMBER>_<PROTOCOL TCP or UDP>

Factors of this structure contain all the past information encoded in URL structure.

One extra environment variable of the structure <ALIAS>_<PORT> will be created and will contain association information for one of the uncovered ports in the URL structure.

These environment factors are accessible for any need application designers may have in connecting to linked containers. In any case, on the off chance that designers have the port and convention predetermined, at that point all they truly need is have name goals and they can depend on DNS for that reason.

Link nature and shortcomings

The nature of links is with the end goal that conditions are directional, static, and nontransitive. Nontransitive implies that linked containers won't inherit links. All the more unequivocally, on the off chance that I link container B to container An, and then link container C to container B, there will be no link from container C to container A.

Links work by determining the system information of a container (IP address and uncovered ports) and then injecting that into another container. Since this is done at container creation time, and Docker can't realize what a container's IP address will be before that container is running, links must be worked from new containers to existing containers. This isn't to say that correspondence is one way but instead that disclosure is one way. This additionally implies if a reliance stops for reasons unknown, the link will be broken. Keep in mind that containers maintain IP address rents just when they're running. So if a container is halted or restarted, it will lose its IP rent and any linked containers will have stale information.

This property has made some censure the estimation of links. The issue is that the more profound a reliance falls flat, the more prominent the domino impact of required container restarts. This may be an issue for a few. However, you should think about the particular effect.

In the event that a basic help like a database falls flat, an accessibility occasion has just happened. The picked administration disclosure technique impacts the recuperation routine. Inaccessible assistance may recoup on the equivalent or different IP address. Links will break just if the IP address changes and will require restarts. This leads some to hop to progressively powerful query systems like DNS.

Yet, even DNS systems have the opportunity to-live (TTL) values that may slow the proliferation of IP address changes. On the off chance that an IP address changes during recuperation, it may feel simpler to utilize DNS, however, recuperation would possibly happen all the more rapidly if associations with the database can fall flat, reconnect endeavors can break, and the DNS TTL lapses in less time than it takes to restart a container. In abandoning container linking, you'll be compelled to empower inter-container correspondence.

On the off chance that your applications are delayed to begin and you have to handle IP address changes on administration recuperation, you might need to consider

DNS. Something else, consider the static reliance chain that has been displayed using container links. Building a system that restarts proper containers on a reliance disappointment would be a feasible exercise.

This part centered around single-have Docker networking, and in that degree links are incredibly helpful apparatuses. Most environments length more than one PC. Administration versatility is the possibility that assistance could be running on any machine, in any container in a more significant environment. The thought a system where any procedure may run anyplace is more strong than systems with severe territory constraints. I think this is valid; however, it's essential to show how Docker can be utilized in either circumstance.

Summary

Networking is a broad subject that would take a few books to cover appropriately. This section should assist perusers with an essential understanding of system basics to receive the single-have networking offices given by Docker. In reading this material, you took in the following:

■ Docker gives four system container models: shut containers, bridged containers, joined containers, and open containers.

■ Docker creates a bridge organize that binds participating containers to one another and to the system that the host is joined to.

■ The bridge interface created by Docker can be supplanted or modified using docker command-line alternatives when the Docker daemon is begun.

■ Options on the docker run command can be utilized to uncover ports on a container's interface, bind ports uncovered by a container to the host's system interface, and link containers to one another.

■ Disabling self-assertive inter-container correspondence is straightforward and manufactures a system with protection top to bottom.

■ Using links gives a low-overhead neighborhood administration revelation instrument and maps specific container conditions.

Limiting risk with isolation

Containers provide an isolated process context. They do not complete system virtualization. The semantic distinction may appear to be inconspicuous; however the effect is extreme. This section will give information on how to improve security on your system.

The features discussed in this chapter focus on managing or mitigating the risk of running software. You will learn how to grant resource permissions to containers, open access to shared memory, run programs as specific users, control what changes the container can make to your computer, and how to integrate with other Linux isolation tools. Some of these topics include Linux features that are beyond the scope of this book. In these cases, I try to give you an idea of its purpose and some basic use cases. You can integrate them into Docker.

Another final reminder, Docker and the technology it uses are developing projects. After finding the learning tools presented in this chapter, be sure to check out developments, improvements, and new best practices when creating something of value.

Resource Allocation

Physical system resources, such as memory and processor time, are scarce. If the consumption of process resources on a computer exceeds the available physical resources, the processes will have performance problems and may stop running. Creating a system that creates strong isolation means allocating resources to individual containers.

If you want to make sure the program does not overwhelm others on your computer, it is easiest to limit the resources you can use. Docker provides three fixed menu execution indicators, and docker creates commands to process three different types of resource allocation that you can place in the container. These three are memory, processor and peripherals.

Memory limitations

Memory constraints are the most basic constraint you can place on a container. They limit the amount of memory that processes in the container can use. Memory constraints are useful to ensure that the container cannot overwrite others in one system. You can set a limit using the -m or - indicator in Docker Run or Docker creates commands. The flag has value and unity. The carpet is as follows:

<number><optional unit>where unit = b, k, m or g

With regards to these commands, b alludes to bytes, k to kilobytes, m to megabytes, and g to gigabytes. Put this new information to utilize and fire up a database application that you'll use in different models:

```
docker run -d --name ch6_mariadb \
--memory 256m \
--cpu-shares 1024

--user nobody \

--cap-drop all \

dockerfile/mariadb
```

With this command, you install database software called MariaDB and start a container with a memory farthest point of 256 megabytes. You may have seen a couple of additional flags on this command. This section covers each of those, yet you may as of now have the option to think about what they do. Something else to note is that you don't uncover any ports or bind any ports to the host's interfaces. It will be least demanding to interface with this database by linking to it from another container. Before we get to that, I need to ensure you have a full understanding of what occurs here and how to utilize memory limits.

The most significant thing to understand about memory limits is that they're not reservations. They don't ensure that the predetermined measure of memory will be profit capable. They're just assurance from overconsumption.

Before you set up a memory remittance, you ought to think about two things. In the first place, can the software you're running work under the proposed memory stipend? Second, can the system you're running on help the recompense?

The primary inquiry is often hard to reply. Rarely to see minimum necessities distributed with open source software nowadays. Regardless of whether it was, however, you'd need to understand how the memory necessities of the software scale dependent on the size of the information you're asking it to handle. Regardless, individuals will in general, overestimate and modify dependent on experimentation. For the situation of memory-touchy apparatuses like databases, gifted professionals, for example, database administrators can improve instructed assessments and suggestions. And still, afterwards, the inquiry is often replied by another: what amount of memory do you have? And that prompts the subsequent inquiry.

Could the system you're running on help the remittance? It's conceivable to set a memory recompense that is greater than the measure of accessible memory on the system. On has that have swap space (virtual memory that expands onto circle), a container may understand the recompense. It's constantly conceivable to force a recompense that is more prominent than any physical memory asset. In those cases the restrictions of the system will consistently top the container.

Finally, understand that there are a few different ways that software can come up short in the event that it depletes the accessible memory. A few programs may come up short with a memory get to blame, while others may begin writing out-of-memory blunders to their logging. Docker neither distinguishes this issue nor endeavors to moderate the issue. All the better it can do is apply the restart rationale you may have determined using the - restart flag portrayed.

CPU

Processing time is similarly as rare as memory; however, the impact of starvation is execution corruption instead of disappointment. A stopped procedure that is waiting for time on the CPU is as yet working accurately. Be that as it may, a moderate procedure might be more awful than a failing one if it's running some significant information processing program, an income-generating web application, or a back-end administration for your application. Docker gives you a chance to restrict a container's CPU assets in two different ways.

To begin with, you can indicate the general load of a container. Linux utilizes this to deflect mine the level of CPU time the container should utilize comparative with other running containers. That rate is for the aggregate of the computing cycles of all processors accessible to the container.

To set the CPU portions of a container and build up its relative weight, both docker run and docker create offer a - CPU-shares flag. The worth ought to be an integer (which implies you shouldn't cite it). Start another container to perceive how CPU shares work:

docker run -d -P --name ch6_wordpress \

--memory 512m \
--cpu-shares 512 \

--user nobody \

--cap-drop net_raw \

--link ch6_mariadb \

wordpress:4.1

This command will download and run WordPress. It is written in PHP and is a great example of software that is challenging to adapt to security risks. Here we begin with some additional precautions. If you want to see it on your computer, use the ch6_wordpress gateway to obtain the port number (port name <port>) on which the service is running and open http: // localhost: <port>. your web browser Remember that if you are using Boot2Docker, you must use boot2docker ip to determine the IP address of the virtual machine on which Docker is running. When available, replace this value with localhost in the previous URL.

When you run the MariaDB container, set its relative weight (CPU units) to 1024 and WordPress to 512. These configurations create a system where the MariaDB container receives two CPU cycles for each WordPress cycle. If you run the third container and set its value - CPU shares in 2048, you will get half of the processing cycle and MariaDB and WordPress will split the other half in the same proportions as before.

CPU stocks differ from memory constraints in that they only apply if there is a time conflict in the CPU. If other processes and tanks are inactive, the container may explode well beyond its limits. This is desirable because it ensures that processor time is not wasted and that limited processes will occur if the processor needs another process. The purpose of this tool is to prevent a process or set of processes from overloading your computer, not to prevent these processes from executing. The default values will not limit the container, and the container can use 100% of the processor.

Another feature that Docker exhibits is the ability to assign a container to a specific set of processors. Most modern hardware uses multi-core processors. The processor can process as many instructions as hearts simultaneously. This is especially useful when running multiple processes on the same computer.

Changing the context is the task of moving from one process to another. Changing context is expensive and can have a significant impact on the performance of your system. In some cases, it may be appropriate to try to minimize the change from text to text by ensuring that critical processes are never performed in the same set of processor cores. You can use the --cpuset-cpus flag when launching a fixed menu or creating a fixed menu to limit the execution of a container in a specific set of processor cores.

You can see the limitations set by the CPU by working on one of the cores of your computer and reviewing its workload:

Start a container limited to a single CPU and run a load generator docker run -d \

--cpuset-cpus 0 \ --name ch6_stresser dockerinaction/ch6_stresser

Start a container to watch the load on the CPU under load docker run -it --rm dockerinaction/ch6_htop

After executing the second command, htop displays the current processes and workload of the available processors. The ch6_stresser tank closes after 30 seconds. Therefore, it is important not to delay the execution of this experiment.

When done with the htop, press Q to exit. Before proceeding, close and remove the container called ch6_stresser:

docker rm -vf ch6_stresser

I thought it was exciting when I first used it. To get the best possible score, repeat this experiment several times using different values for the --cpuset-cpus indicator. If this happens, the procedure will be assigned to different hearts or different sets of hearts. The value can be in the form of a list or range:

- 0,1,2: A list that includes the first three CPU cores

- 0-2: range that includes the first three CPU cores

Access to devices

Devices are the last type of resource. This control is different from the memory constraints and the processor in that access to devices is not a limit. It's more like checking the permission of a resource.

Linux systems have all kinds of peripherals, including hard drives, optical drives, USB drives, a mouse, keyboard, audio devices, and webcams. Containers have access to some of these default devices, and Docker creates others for each container (such as virtual terminals).

Occasionally, it may be important to share other devices between the host and the specified container. Imagine a situation where you run computer vision software that requires webcam access. In this case, you must grant access to the container that runs your software to the webcam device connected to the system. You can use the --digit flag to specify a set of devices to install in a new container. The following example assigns your webcam located in / dev / video0 the same location in a new container. Running this example will only work if you have a webcam in / dev / video0:

```
docker -it --rm \
--device / dev / video0: / dev / video0 \
ubuntu: last ls -al / dev
```

The specified value must be a map between the device file in the host operating system and the location in the new container. The device indicator can be set several times to allow access to different devices.

People with custom hardware or their own drivers will find this type of access useful for devices. It's better to modify your home operating system.

Shared memory

Linux provides some tools for sharing memory between processes running on the same computer. This form of inter-process communication (IPC) operates at memory speed. It is often used when a delay associated with a network or pipe based on CPI results in software performance of less than the requirement. Best examples of sharing

Memory-based CPIs are used in scientific computing and some popular database technologies, such as PostgreSQL.

Docker creates a default unique IPC space for each container. Linux IPC partition names share primitive memories, such as shared memory blocks with names and semaphores, as well as message queues. It doesn't matter if you are not sure what they are. Note that these are the tools that Linux programs use to coordinate processing. The IPC namespace prevents processes in the container from accessing memory on the host or other containers.

Divide IPC primitives between containers

I created an image called dockerinactionch6_ipc that contains both the manufacturer and the consumer. They communicate using shared memory. The following will help you understand the problem of running in separate containers:

docker -d -u person - name ch6_ipc_producer \
dockerinaction / ch6_ipc -producer
docker -d -u person - name ch6_ipc_consumer \
dockerinaction / ch6_ipc - Consumer

These commands start two containers. The first creates a message line and begins broadcasting messages on it. The second should pull from the message line and compose the messages to the logs. You can perceive what each is doing by using the following commands to inspect the logs of each:

docker logs ch6_ipc_producer

docker logs ch6_ipc_consumer

Notice that something isn't right with the containers you began. The purchaser never observes any messages on the line. Each procedure utilized a similar key to recognize the mutual memory asset, however they alluded to different memory. The explanation is that every container has its very own common memory namespace.

On the off chance that you have to run programs that communicate with shared memory in different containers, at that point you'll have to join their IPC namespaces with the - ipc banner. The - ipc banner has a container mode that will create another container in the equivalent IPC namespace as another objective container.

Utilize the following commands to test joined IPC namespaces for yourself:

docker rm - v ch6_ipc_consumer

docker - d - name ch6_ipc_consumer \

- ipc container:ch6_ipc_producer \

dockerinaction/ch6_ipc - buyer

These commands revamp the buyer container and reuse the IPC namespace of the ch6_ipc_producer container. This time the shopper ought to have the option to get to the same memory area where the server is writing. You can see that it works by using the following commands to view each other's records:

docker log ch6_ipc_producer

docker log ch6_ipc_consumer

Make sure to tidy up your running containers before moving on:

■ The v choice will tidy up volumes.

■ The f choice will slaughter the container on the off chance that it is running.

■ The rm command takes a rundown of containers.

docker rm - vf ch6_ipc_producer ch6_ipc_consumer

There are clear security ramifications to reusing the common memory namespaces of containers. In any case, this alternative is available in case you need it. Sharing memory between containers is a more secure option than sharing a memory with the host.

Using an open memory container

Memory disengagement is an attractive quality. If you experience a circumstance where you have to work in the equivalent namespace as the remainder of the host, you can do so using an open memory container:

docker - d - name ch6_ipc_producer \

- ipc have \

dockerinaction/ch6_ipc – maker

docker - d - name ch6_ipc_consumer \- - ipc have \dockerinaction/ch6_ipc - customer

These containers will have the option to communicate with one another and some other procedures running on the host PC right away. As should be obvious in this model, you empower this element by specifying host on the - ipc banner. You may utilize this in situations when you have to communicate with a procedure that must sudden spike in demand for the host, yet as a rule you should attempt to keep away from this if conceivable.

 Feel free to check the source code for this model. It's a revolting yet straightforward C program. You can find it by checking out the source storehouse linked to from the picture's page on Docker Hub.

You can tidy up the containers you created in this segment using a similar cleanup command

docker rm - vf ch6_ipc_producer ch6_ipc_consumer

Open memory containers are a hazard, yet it's a much better plan to utilize them than to run those procedures outside a container.

Understanding users

Docker begins containers as the root client inside that container as a matter of course. The root client has practically full special access to the condition of the container. Any procedures running as that client inherit those authorizations. It pursues that if there's a bug in one of those procedures, they may harm the container. There are approaches to constrain the harm, however the best method to counteract these kinds of issues isn't to utilize the root client.

There are sensible special cases when using the root client is the best if not just accessible alternative. You utilize the root client for building images and at runtime when there's no other alternative. There are other comparative circumstances when you need to run system administration software inside a container. In those cases, the procedure needs advantaged access not exclusively to the container yet additionally to the host operating system. This area covers the scope of answers for these issues.

Introduction to the Linux client namespace

Linux as of late discharged another client (USR) namespace that permits users in one namespace to be mapped to users in another. The new namespace works like the procedure identifier (PID) namespace.

Docker is not yet integrated into the US namespace. This implies that the container that works with the client ID (number, not name) equivalent to the client on the host device has permissions of the host file similar to that of the client. This isn't an issue. The file system accessible inside a container has been mounted so that changes that are made inside that container will remain inside that container's file system. Be that as it may, this impacts volumes.

At the point when Docker embraces the USR namespace, you'll have the option to outline IDs on the host to client IDs in a container namespace. In this way, I could delineate 1000 on my host to client 2 in the container. This is especially valuable for resolving file authorizations issues in cases like reading and writing to volumes.

Working with the run-as client

Before you create a container, it is decent to have the option to determine what username (and client ID) will be utilized as a matter of course. The picture indicates the default. There's right now no real way to examine a picture to find traits like the default client. This information isn't included on Docker Hub. And there's no command to examine picture metadata.

The nearest include accessible is the docker inspect command. If you missed before, the inspect subcommand shows the metadata of a particular container. Container metadata includes the metadata of the picture it was created from. When you've created a container—how about we call it sway—you can get the username that the container is using with the following commands:

docker create - name weave busybox: latest ping localhost

docker inspect weave

docker inspect - - group "{{.Config.User}}" bounce

On the off chance that the outcome is clear, the container will default to running as the root client. In the event that it isn't clear, either the picture creator explicitly named a default run-as client or you set a particular run-as client when you created the container. The - position or - f alternative utilized in the subsequent command enables you to determine a format to render the yield. For this situation, you've chosen the User field of the Config property of the archive. The worth can be any legitimate GoLang format, so in case you're feeling ready, you can get inventive with the outcomes.

There are issues with this methodology. To start with, the run-as client may be changed by whatever content the picture uses to fire up. These are now and again alluded to as boot or init contents. The metadata returned by docker inspect includes just the setup that the container was begun with. So if the client transforms, it won't be reflected there. Second, you need to create a container from a picture in request to get the information. That can be risky.

Right now, the best way to fix the two issues is look inside the picture. You could expand the picture files after you download them and examine the metadata and init contents by hand, however doing so is tedious and simple to get off-base. For the present, it might be smarter to run a straightforward examination to determine the default client. This will tackle the primary issue however not the second:

docker run - - rm - - entrypoint "" busybox:latest whoami

docker run - - rm - - entrypoint "" busybox:latest id

This exhibits two commands that you may use to determine the default client of a picture (for this situation, busybox:latest). Both the whoami and id commands are com-mon among Linux conveyances, and so they're probably going to be accessible in some random picture. The subsequent command is prevalent because it shows both the name and ID subtleties for the run-as client. Both these commands are mindful to unset the entrypoint of the container. This will ensure that the command indicated after the picture name is the command that is executed by the container. These are poor substitutes for a top of the line picture metadata apparatus, yet they take care of business.

You can completely maintain a strategic distance from the default client issue if you change the run-as client when you create the container. The idiosyncrasy with using this is the username must exist on the picture you're using. Different Linux circulations send with different users predefined, and some picture creators diminish or increase that set. You can get a rundown of accessible users in a picture with the following command:

docker run - rm busybox:latest awk - F: '$0=$1'/and so forth/passwd

I won't broadly expound here; however the Linux client database is put away in a file situated at/and so on/passwd. This command will peruse that file and draw a rundown of the usernames. When you've recognized the client you need to utilize, you can create another container with a particular run-as client. Docker gives the - client or - u banner on docker run and docker create for setting the client. This will set the client to "no one":

```
docker run - - rm \
```

```
- user nobody \
```

```
busybox:latest id
```

This command utilized the "no one" client. That client is normal and intended for use in confined benefits situations like running applications. That was only one model. You can utilize any username defined by the picture here, including root. This solitary starts to expose what you can do with the - u or - client banner. The worth can acknowledge any client or gathering pair. It can likewise acknowledge client and gathering names or IDs. At the point when you use IDs instead of names, the choices begin to open up:

Users and volumes

Now that you've learned how users inside containers share the same user ID space as the users on your host system, you need to learn how those two might interact. The main reason for that interaction is the file permissions on files in volumes. For example, if you're running a Linux terminal, you should be able to use these commands directly; otherwise, you'll need to use the boot2docker ssh command to get a shell in your Boot2Docker virtual machine:

```
        echo "e=mc^2" > garbage
    chmod 600 garbage
    sudo chown root:root garbage

        docker run --rm -v "$(pwd)"/garbage:/test/garbage \
        -u nobody \
        ubuntu:latest cat /test/garbage
        docker run --rm -v "$(pwd)"/garbage:/test/garbage \
        -u root ubuntu:latest cat /test/garbage

        # Outputs: "e=mc^2"
    #cleanup that garbage sudo rm -f garbage
```

The second-to-last docker command should fail with an error message like "Permission denied." But the last docker command should succeed and show you the con-tents of the file you created in the first command. This means that file permissions on files in volumes are respected inside the container. But this also reflects that the user ID space is shared. Both root on the host and root in the container have user ID 0. So, although the container's nobody user with ID 65534 can't access a file owned by root on the host, the container's root user can.

Unless you want a file to be accessible to a container, don't mount it into that con-tainer with a volume.

The good news about this example is that you've seen how file permissions are respected and can solve some more mundane—but practical—operational issues. For example, how do you handle a log file written to a volume?

The preferred way is with volume containers. But even then you need to consider file ownership and permission issues. If logs are written to a volume by a process running as user 1001 and another container tries to access that file as user 1002, then file permissions might prevent the operation.

One way to overcome this obstacle would be to specifically manage the user ID of the running user. You can either edit the image ahead of time by setting the user ID of the user you're going to run the container with, or you can use the desired user and group ID:

```
mkdir logFiles

sudo chown 2000:2000 logFiles

docker run --rm -v "$(pwd)"/logFiles:/logFiles \
-u 2000:2000 ubuntu:latest \

/bin/bash -c "echo This is important info > /logFiles/important.log"
docker run --rm -v "$(pwd)"/logFiles:/logFiles \

-u 2000:2000 ubuntu:latest \ /bin/bash -c "echo More info >> /logFiles/important.log"

sudo rm –r logFiles
```

After running this example, you'll see that the file could be written to the directory that's owned by user 2000. Not only that, but any container that uses a user or group with write access to the directory could write a file in that directory or to the same file if the permissions allow. This trick works for reading, writing, and executing files.

Adjusting OS feature access with capabilities

Docker can adjust the feature authorization of processes within containers. In Linux these feature authorizations are called capabilities, but as native support expands to other operating systems, other back-end implementations would need to be provided. Whenever a process attempts to make a gated system call, the capabilities of that process are checked for the required capability. The call will succeed if the process has the required capability and fail otherwise.

When you create a new container, Docker drops a specific set of capabilities by default. This is done to further isolate the running process from the administrative functions of the operating system. In reading this list of dropped capabilities, you might be able to guess at the reason for their removal. At the time of this writing, this set includes the following:

- SETPCAP—Modify process capabilities

- SYS_MODULE—Insert/remove kernel modules

- SYS_RAWIO—Modify kernel memory

- SYS_PACCT—Configure process accounting

- SYS_NICE—Modify priority of processes

- SYS_RESOURCE—Override resource limits

- SYS_TIME—Modify the system clock

- SYS_TTY_CONFIG—Configure TTY devices

- AUDIT_WRITE—Write the audit log

- AUDIT_CONTROL—Configure audit subsystem

- MAC_OVERRIDE—Ignore kernel MAC policy

- MAC_ADMIN—Configure MAC configuration

- SYSLOG—Modify kernel print behavior

- NET_ADMIN—Configure the network

- SYS_ADMIN—Catchall for administrative functions

The default set of capabilities provided to Docker containers provides a reasonable feature reduction, but there will be times when you need to add or reduce this set fur-ther. For example, the capability NET_RAW can be dangerous. If you wanted to be a bit more careful than the default configuration, you could drop NET_RAW from the list of capabilities. You can drop capabilities from a container using the --cap-drop flag on docker create or docker run.

```
docker run --rm -u nobody \

ubuntu:latest \

/bin/bash -b"capsh --print | grep net_raw"

docker run --rm -u nobody \

--cap-drop net_raw \

ubuntu:latest \

/bin/bash -b "capsh --print | grep net_raw"
```

In Linux documentation you'll often see capabilities named in all uppercase and prefixed with CAP_, but that prefix won't work if provided to the capability-management options. Use unprefixed and lowercase names for the best results.

Similar to the --cap-drop flag, the --cap-add flag will add capabilities. If you needed to add the SYS_ADMIN capability for some reason, you'd use a command like the following:

```
docker run --rm -u nobody \
ubuntu:latest \
/bin/bash –b "capsh --print | grep sys_admin"

docker run --rm -u nobody \
--cap-add sys_admin \

ubuntu:latest \

/bin/bash –b "capsh --print | grep sys_admin"
```

Like other container-creation options, both --cap-add and --cap-drop can be specified multiple times to add or drop multiple capabilities. These flags can be used to build containers that will let a process perform exactly and only what is required for proper operation.

Running a container with full privileges

In those cases when you need to run a system administration task inside a container, you can grant that container privileged access to your computer. Privileged containers maintain their file system and network isolation but have full access to shared memory and devices and possess full system capabilities. You can perform several interesting tasks, like running Docker inside a container, with privileged containers.

The bulk of the uses for privileged containers is administrative. Take, for example, an environment where the root file system is read-only, or installing software outside a container has been disallowed, or you have no direct access to a shell on the host. If you wanted to run a program to tune the operating system (for something like load balancing) and you had access to run a container on that host, then you could simply run that program in a privileged container.

If you find a situation that can be solved only with the reduced isolation of a privileged container, use the --privileged flag on docker create or docker run to enable this mode:

```
docker run --rm \
--privileged \
ubuntu:latest id

docker run --rm \

--privileged \

ubuntu:latest capsh –print

docker run --rm \

--privileged \

ubuntu:latest ls /dev

docker run --rm \

--privileged \

ubuntu:latest ifconfig
```

Privileged containers are still partially isolated. For example, the network namespace will still be in effect. If you need to tear down that namespace, you'll need to combine this with --net host as well.

Stronger containers with enhanced tools

Docker uses reasonable defaults and a "batteries included" toolset to ease adoption and promote best practices. But you can enhance the containers it builds if you bring additional tools. Tools you can use to harden your containers include AppArmor and SELinux. If you use the LXC container provider, you can also provide custom LXC con-figuration and get into fine-tuning containers. If you're using LXC, you can even use a Linux feature called seccomp-bpf (secure computing with system call filtering).

They bring their own nuances, benefits, and required skillsets. Their use is—without question—worth the effort. Support for each varies by Linux distribution, so you may be in for a bit of work. But once you've adjusted your host configuration, the Docker integration is simpler.

Specifying additional security options

Docker provides a single flag for specifying options for Linux Security Modules (LSM) at container creation or runtime. LSM is a framework that Linux adapted to act as an interface layer between the operating system and security providers.

AppArmor and SELinux are both LSM providers. They both provide mandatory access control (MAC—the system defines access rules) and replace the standard Linux discretionary access control (file owners define access rules).

The flag available on docker run and Docker create --security-opt. This flag can be set multiple times to pass multiple values. The values can currently be one of six formats:

- To set a SELinux user label, use the form label:user:<USERNAME> where <USERNAME> is the name of the user you want to use for the label.

- To set a SELinux role label, use the form label:role:<ROLE> where <ROLE> is the name of the role you want to apply to processes in the container.

- To set a SELinux type label, use the form label:type:<TYPE> where <TYPE> is the type name of the processes in the container.

- To set a SELinux level label, use the form label:level:<LEVEL> where <LEVEL> is the level where processes in the container should run. Levels are specified as low-high pairs. Where abbreviated to the low level only, SELinux will interpret the range as single level.

- To disable SELinux label confinement for a container, use the form label:disable.

- To apply an AppArmor profile on the container, use the form label:apparmor:<PROFILE> where <PROFILE> is the name of the AppArmor profile to use.

As you can guess from these options, SELinux is a labeling system. A set of labels, called a *context*, is applied to every file and system object. A similar set of labels is applied to every user and process. At runtime when a process attempts to interact with a file or system resource, the sets of labels are evaluated against a set of allowed rules. The result of that evaluation determines whether the interaction is allowed or blocked.

The last option will set an AppArmor profile. AppArmor is frequently substituted for SELinux because it works with file paths instead of labels and has a training mode that you can use to passively build profiles based on observed application behavior. These differences are often cited as reasons why AppArmor is easier to adopt and maintain.

Fine-tuning with LXC

Docker was originally built to use a software called Linux Containers (LXC). LXC is a container runtime provider—a tool that actually works with Linux to create namespaces and all the components that go into building a container.

As Docker matured and portability became a concern, a new container runtime called libcontainer was built, replacing LXC. Docker ships with libcontainer by default, but Docker uses an interface layer so that users can change the container exe-cution provider. LXC is a more mature library than libcontainer and provides many additional features that diverge from the goals of Docker. If you're running a system where you can and want to use LXC, you can change the container provider and take advantage of those additional features. Before investing too heavily, know that some of those additional features will greatly reduce the portability of your containers.

To use LXC, you need to install it and make sure the Docker daemon was started with the LXC driver enabled. Use the --exec-driver=lxc option when you start the Docker daemon. The daemon is usually configured to start as one of your system's ser-vices. Check the installation instructions on www.docker.com to find details for your distribution.

Once Docker is configured for LXC, you can use the --lxc-conf flag on docker run or Docker create to set the LXC configuration for a container:

docker

```
run
-d \

--lxc-conf="lxc.cgroup.cpuset.cpus=0,1" \

--name
ch6_stresser dockerinaction/ch6_stresser

docker
run
-it --rm dockerinaction/ch6_htop

docker rm -vf ch6_stresser
```

As when you ran a similar example earlier in this chapter, when you've finished with htop, press Q to quit.

If you decide to use the LXC provider and specify LXC-specific options for your containers, Docker won't be aware of that configuration. Certain configurations can be provided that conflict with the standard container changes made for every Docker container. For this reason, you should always carefully validate the configuration against the actual impact of a container.

Build tanks customized for use in cases

Containers are the most important issues. Reasons and ways for people to use them more than I could list. Therefore, it is important when you use Docker to create a container for your use that you take the time to do so appropriately for the software you are running.

The surest tactic to do this would be to start with the most insulated tank you can build and justify the reasons why these restrictions are weakened. In reality, people tend to be a little more reactive than proactive. Which is why I think Docker finds a good compromise with the default container build. Provide reasonable default values without compromising user productivity.

Docker containers are not the most disengaged of course. Docker does not require you to improve these defaults. This will allow you to do production nonsense if you wish. Because of this, Docker looks a lot more like a tool than a burden and is something that people mostly want to use instead of feeling compelled to do so. For those who do not want to do the nonsense of manufacturing, Docker offers a simple interface to improve tank insulation.

Applications

Applicaions are the reason we use computers. Most applications are programs written by other people and use potentially malicious data. Think about your web browser.

A web browser is an example of a program installed on almost all computers. Communicate with web sites, images, scripts, embedded videos, Flash documents, Java applications and more. You certainly didn't create all this content, and most people didn't contribute to web browser projects. How can you trust your web browser to manage all this content properly?

Well, if an attacker takes control of your web browser (or any other application), you will benefit from all the features of this application and the permission of the user running it. They can destroy your computer, delete your files, install other malware, or even launch attacks on other computers from your computer. Therefore, it is not good to ignore it. The question remains: how do you protect yourself when it comes to the risk you should take?

The best approach is to isolate risk. First, make sure the app works as a restricted user. As a result, files on your computer cannot be modified in the event of a problem. Second, limit the capabilities of your browser system. This ensures that your system configuration is more secure. Third, configure the amount of CPU and memory the application can use. Restrictions can reserve resources so that the system can continue to respond. Lastly, it's a good idea to mark the devices you can access specifically. This will save snipers from your webcam, USB, etc.

High-level system services

High-level system services are slightly different from applications. They are not part of the operating system, but your computer makes sure they are up and running. These tools often come with applications outside the operating system but often require privileged access to the operating system to function properly. They provide important functionality to users and other software in the system. Examples include cron, syslogd, dbus, sshd, and docker.

If you do not know these tools (hopefully not all), then everything is fine. They do things like keep system logs, execute scheduled commands, and provide a way to get a secure shell on the system from the network while Docker manages the containers.

Although the provision of services as a root user is common, some require full privileged access. Use functions to customize your access to the specific functions you need.

Low-level system services

Low-level services control things like a device or a bundle of network power. They require privileged access to the delivered system components (for example, firewall software requires administrative access to a network set).

It's weird to see them running in containers. Tasks such as file system administration, device administration, and network administration are the central concerns of the host. Most software that runs in containers must be portable. Because of this, specific machine tasks like these are not generally for use with tanks.

The best exceptions are short-lived configuration containers. For example, in an environment where all implementations take place with images and Docker containers, you do not want to apply changes to the network stack in the same way as with software. In this case, you can pass the configuration image to the host and make changes with the privileged container. In this case, the risk is reduced because you created the insertion configuration, the container does not run for a long time and changes like these are easily audited.

Summary

This chapter introduces the isolation features provided by Linux and explains how Docker uses them to create configurable containers. Thanks to this knowledge, you can customize the container insulation and use Docker in all use cases. This chapter deals with the following points:

■ Docker uses control groups that allow the user to set memory limits, processor weights, and major processor limitations, as well as restrict access to specific devices.

■ Each Docker container has its own IPC namespace that can be shared with other containers or with the host to facilitate shared memory communication.

Build automation and advanced image considerations

A Dockerfile is a Doc that contains instructions for building an image. The instructions are followed by the Docker image builder from top to bottom and can be used to change anything about an image. Building images from Dockerfiles makes tasks like adding files to a container from your computer simple one-line instructions. This part covers the basics of working with Dockerfile builds and the best reasons to use them, a lean overview of the instructions, and how to add future build behavior. We'll get started with a familiar example.

Packaging Git with a Dockerfile

Let's start by revisiting the Git on Ubuntu example. Having previously built a similar image by hand, you should recognize many of the details and advantages of working with a Dockerfile.

First, create a new directory and from that directory create a new file with your favorite text editor. Name the new file Dockerfile. Write the following five lines and then save the file:

An example Dockerfile for installing Git on Ubuntu FROM ubuntu:latest

MAINTAINER "dockerinaction@allingeek.com" RUN apt-get install -y git

ENTRYPOINT ["git"]

Before dissecting this example, build a new image from it with the docker build command from the same directory containing the Dockerfile. Tag the new image with auto:

```
docker build --tag ubuntu-git:auto .
```

Outputs several lines about steps and output from apt-get and will finally display a message like this:

```
Successfully built 0bca8436849b
```

Running this command starts the build process. When it's completed, you should have a brand-new image that you can test. View the list of all your ubuntu-git images and test the newest one with this command:

```
docker images
```

The new build tagged "auto" should now appear in the list:

```
REPOSITORY
TAG
IMAGE ID
CREATED
VIRTUAL SIZE

ubuntu-git
auto
0bca8436849b
10
seconds ago
225.9
MB

ubuntu-git
latest
826c66145a59
10
minutes ago
226.6
MB
```

ubuntu-git
removed
826c66145a59
10
minutes ago
226.6
MB

ubuntu-git
1.9
3e356394c14e
41
hours ago
226 MB

...

Now you can run a Git command using the new image:

docker run --rm ubuntu-git:auto

These commands demonstrate that the image you built with the Dockerfile works and is functionally equivalent to the one you built by hand. Examine what you did to accomplish this:

First, you created a Dockerfile with four instructions:

■ FROM ubuntu:latest—Tells Docker to start from the latest Ubuntu image just as you did when creating the image manually.

■ MAINTAINER—Sets the maintainer name and email for the image. Providing this information helps people know who to contact if there's a problem with the image. This was accomplished earlier when you invoked commit.

■ RUN apt-get install –y git—Tells the builder to run the provided com-mand to install Git.

■ ENTRYPOINT ["git"]—Sets the entrypoint for the image to git.

Dockerfiles, like most scripts, can include comments. The builder will ignore any line beginning with a #. Dockerfiles of any complexity needs to be well documented. In addition to improving Dockerfile maintainability, comments help people audit images that they're considering for adoption and spread best practices.

The only special rule about Dockerfiles is that the first instruction must be FROM. If you're starting from an empty image and your software has no dependencies, or you'll provide all the dependencies, then you can start from a special empty repository named scratch.

After you saved the Dockerfile, you started the build process by invoking the docker build command. The command had one flag set and one argument. The --tag flag (or -t for short) specifies the full repository designation that you want to use for the resulting image. In this case, you used ubuntu-git: auto. The argument that you included at the end was a single period. That argument told the builder the location of the Dockerfile. The period told it to look for the file in the current directory.

The docker build command has another flag, --file (or -f for short), that lets you set the name of the Dockerfile. Dockerfile is the default, but with this flag you could tell the builder to look for a file named BuildScript. This flag sets only the name of the file, not the location of the file. That must always be specified in the location argument.

The builder works by automating the same tasks that you'd use to create images by hand. Each instruction triggers the creation of a new container with the specified modification. After the modification has been made, the builder commits the layer and moves on to the next instruction and container created from the fresh layer.

The builder validated that the image specified by the FROM instruction was installed as the first step of the build. If it were not, Docker would have automatically tried to pull the image. Take a look at the output from the build command that you ran:

Sending build context to Docker daemon 2.058 kB

Sending build context to Docker daemon

Step 0 : FROM ubuntu:latest

---> b39b81afc8ca

You can see that for this situation the base picture indicated by the FROM guidance is ubuntu:latest, which ought to have just been introduced on your machine. The abridged picture ID of the base picture is remembered for the yield.

The next instruction sets the maintainer information on the image. This creates a new container and then commits the resulting layer. You can see the result of this operation in the output for step 1:

Step 1: MAINTAINER "dockerinaction@allingeek.com."

---> Running in 938ff06bf8f4

---> 80a695671201

Removing intermediate container 938ff06bf8f4

The output includes the ID of the container that was created and the ID of the committed layer. That layer will be used as the top of the image for the next instruction, RUN. The output for the RUN instruction was clouded with all the output for the com-mand apt-get install -y git. If you're not interested in this output, you can invoke the docker build command with the --quiet or -q flag. Running in quiet mode will suppress output from the intermediate containers. Without the container output, the RUN step produces output that looks like this:

Step 2: RUN apt-get install -y git

---> Running in 4438c3b2c049

---> 1c20f8970532

Removing intermediate container 4438c3b2c049

Although this step usually takes much longer to complete, you can see the instruction and input as well as the ID of the container where the command was run and the ID of the resulting layer. Finally, the ENTRYPOINT instruction performs all the same steps, and the output is similarly unsurprising:

Step 3: ENTRYPOINT git

---> Running in c9b24b0f035c

---> 89d726cf3514

Removing intermediate container c9b24b0f035c

A new layer is being added to the resulting image after each step in the build. Although this means you could potentially branch on any of these steps, the more important implication is that the builder can aggressively cache the results of each step. If a problem with the build script occurs after several other steps, the builder can restart from the same position after the problem has been fixed. You can see this in action by breaking your Dockerfile.

Add this line to the end of your Dockerfile:

RUN This will not work

Then rerun the build:

docker build --tag ubuntu-git:auto.

The output will show which steps the builder was able to skip in favor of cached results:

Sending build context to Docker daemon 2.058 kB Sending build context to Docker daemon

Step 0 : FROM ubuntu:latest

---> b39b81afc8ca

Step 1 : MAINTAINER "dockerinaction@allingeek.com"

---> Using cache

---> 80a695671201

Step 2: RUN apt-get install -y git

Note use of cache

---> Using cache

---> 1c20f8970532

Step 3: ENTRYPOINT git

---> Using cache

---> 89d726cf3514

Step 4: RUN This will not work

---> Running in f68f0e0418b5

/bin/sh: 1: This: not found

INFO[0001] The command [/bin/sh -c This will not work] returned a non-zero code: 127

Steps 1 through 3 were skipped because they were already built during your last build. Step 4 failed because there's no program with the name This in the container. The container output was valuable in this case because the error message informs you about the specific problem with the Dockerfile. If you fix the problem, the same steps will be skipped again, and the build will succeed, resulting in output like Successfully built d7a8ee0cebd4.

The use of caching during the build can save time if the build includes download-ing material, compiling programs, or anything else that is time-intense. If you need a full rebuild, you can use the --no-cache flag on docker build to disable the use of the cache. But make sure you're disabling the cache only when absolutely required.

This short example uses 4 of the 14 Dockerfile instructions. The example was lim-ited in that all the files that were added to the image were downloaded from the network; it modified the environment in a very limited way and provided a very gen-eral tool. The next example with a more specific purpose and local code will provide a more complete Dockerfile primer.

Dockerfiles are expressive and easy to understand due to their terse syntax that allows for comments. You can keep track of changes to Dockerfiles with any version-control system. Maintaining multiple versions of an image is as simple as keeping dockerfiles multiple. The Dockerfile build process itself uses extensive caching to aid rapid development and iteration. The builds are traceable and reproducible. They integrate easily with existing build systems and many continuous build and integration tools. With all these reasons to prefer Dockerfile builds to hand-made images, it's important to learn how to write them.

The examples in this section cover each of the Dockerfile instructions except for one. The ONBUILD instruction has a specific use case and is covered in the next section. Every instruction is covered here at an introductory level. For deep coverage of each instruction, the best reference will always be the Docker documentation. online at https://docs.docker.com/reference/builder/. Docker also provides a best practices section in its documentation: http://docs.docker.com/reference/builder.

Metadata instructions

The first example builds a base image and two other images with distinct versions of the mailer program. The purpose of the program is to listen for messages on a TCP port and then send those messages to their intended recipients. The first version of the mailer will listen for messages but only log those messages. The second will send the message as an HTTP POST to the defined URL.

One of the best reasons to use Dockerfile builds is that they simplify copying files from your computer into an image. But it's not always appropriate for certain files to be copied to images. The first thing to do when starting a new project is to define which files should never be copied into any images. You can do this in a file called

.dockerignore. In this example you'll be creating three Dockerfiles, and none needs to be copied into the resulting images.

Use your favorite text editor to create a new file named .dockerignore and copy in the following lines:

.dockerignore

mailer-base.df

mailer-logging.df

mailer-live.df

Save and close the file when you've finished. This will prevent the .dockerignore file, or files named mailer-base.df, mailer-log.df, or mailer-live.df, from ever being copied into an image during a build. With that bit of accounting finished, you can begin working on the base image.

Building a base image helps create common layers. Each of the different versions of the mailer will be built on top of an image called mailer-base. When you create a Dockerfile, you need to keep in mind that each Dockerfile instruction will result in a new layer being created. Instructions should be combined whenever possible because the builder won't perform any optimization. Putting this in practice, create a new file named mailer-base.df and add the following lines:

FROM debian:wheezy

MAINTAINER Jeff Nickoloff "dia@allingeek.com"

RUN groupadd -r -g 2200 example && \

  useradd -rM -g example -u 2200 example

ENV APPROOT="/app" \

  APP="mailer.sh" \

VERSION="0.6"

LABEL base.name="Mailer Archetype" \
base.version="${VERSION}"

WORKDIR $APPROOT
This file does

ADD . $APPROOT

not exist yet

ENTRYPOINT ["/app/mailer.sh"]

EXPOSE 33333

Do not set the default user in the base otherwise
implementations will not be able to update the image

USER example:example

Put it all together by running the docker build command from the directory where the mailer-base file is located. The -f flag tells the builder which filename to use as input:

docker build -t dockerinaction/mailer-base:0.6 -f mailer-base.df .

Five new instructions are introduced in this Dockerfile. The first new instruction is ENV. ENV sets environment variables for an image similar to the --env flag on docker run or docker create. In this case, a single ENV instruction is used to set three distinct environment variables. That could have been accomplished with three subsequent ENV instructions, but doing so would result in the creation of three layers. You can keep things looking well structured by using a backslash to escape the newline charac-ter (just like shell scripting):

Step 3 : ENV APPROOT "/app" APP "mailer.sh" VERSION "0.6"

---> Running in 05cb87a03b1b

---> 054f1747aa8d

Removing intermediate container 05cb87a03b1b

Environment variables declared in the Dockerfile are made available to the resulting image but can be used in other Dockerfile instructions as substitutions. In this Dockerfile the environment variable VERSION was used as a substitution in the next new instruction, LABEL:

Step 4 : LABEL base.name "Mailer Archetype" base.version "${VERSION}"

---> Running in 0473087065c4

---> ab76b163e1d7

Removing intermediate container 0473087065c4

The LABEL instruction is used to define key/value pairs that are recorded as additional metadata for an image or container. This mirrors the --label flag on docker run and docker create. Like the ENV instruction before it, multiple labels can and should be set with a single instruction. In this case, the value of the VERSION environment vari-able was substituted for the value of the base.version label. By using an environment variable in this way, the value of VERSION will be available to processes running inside a container as well as recorded to an appropriate label. This increases maintainability of the Dockerfile because it's more difficult to make inconsistent changes when the value is set in a single location.

The next two instructions are WORKDIR and EXPOSE. These are similar in operation to their corresponding flags on the docker run and docker create commands. An environment variable was substituted for the argument to the WORKDIR command:

Step 5: WORKDIR $APPROOT

---> Running in 073583e0d554

---> 363129ccda97

Removing intermediate container 073583e0d554

The result of the WORKDIR instruction will be an image with the default working direc-tory set to /app. Setting WORKDIR to a location that doesn't exist will create that location just like the command-line option. Last, the EXPOSE command creates a layer that opens TCP port 33333:

Step 7: EXPOSE 33333

---> Running in a6c4f54b2907

---> 86e0b43f234a

Removing intermediate container a6c4f54b2907

The parts of this Dockerfile that you should recognize are the FROM, MAINTAINER, and ENTRYPOINT instructions. In brief, the FROM instruction sets the layer stack to start from the debian: wheezy image. Any new layers built will be placed on top of that image. The MAINTAINER instruction sets the Author value in the image metadata. The ENTRYPOINT instruction sets the executable to be run at container startup. Here, it's set-ting the instruction to exec ./mailer.sh and using the shell form of the instruction.

The ENTRYPOINT instruction has two forms: the shell form and an exec form. The shell form looks like a shell command with whitespace-delimited arguments. The exec form is a string array where the first value is the command to execute and the remain-ing values are arguments. A command specified using the shell form would be executed as an argument to the default shell. Specifically, the command used in this Dockerfile will be executed as /bin/sh –c 'exec ./mailer.sh' at runtime. Most importantly, if the shell form is used for ENTRYPOINT, then all other arguments pro-vided by the CMD instruction or at runtime as extra arguments to docker run will be ignored. This makes the shell form of ENTRYPOINT less flexible.

You can see from the build output that the ENV and LABEL instructions each resulted in a single step and layer. But the output doesn't show that the environment variable values were substituted correctly. To verify that, you'll need to inspect the image:

docker inspect dockerinaction/mailer-base:0.6

TIP Remember, the docker inspect command can be used to view the metadata of either a container or an image. In this case, you used it to inspect an image.

The relevant lines are these:

"Env": [

"PATH=/usr/local/sbin:/usr/local/bin:/usr/sbin:/usr/bin:/sbin:/bin",

```
"APPROOT=/app",

"APP=mailer.sh",

"VERSION=0.6"

],

...

"Labels": {

"base.name": "Mailer Archetype",

"base.version": "0.6"

},

...

"WorkingDir": "/app"
```

The metadata makes it clear that the environment variable substitution works. You can use this form of substitution in the ENV, ADD, COPY, WORKDIR, VOLUME, EXPOSE, and USER instructions.

The last commented line is a metadata instruction USER. It sets the user and group for all further build steps and containers created from the image. In this case, setting it in a base image would prevent any downstream Dockerfiles from installing software. That would mean that those Dockerfiles would need to flip the default back and forth for permission. Doing so would create at least two additional layers. The better approach would be to set up the user and group accounts in the base image and let the implementations set the default user when they've finished building.

The most curious thing about this Dockerfile is that the ENTRYPOINT is set to a file that doesn't exist. The entrypoint will fail when you try to run a container from this base image. But now that the entrypoint is set in the base image, that's one less layer that will need to be duplicated for specific implementations of the mailer. The next two Dockerfiles build mailer.sh different implementations.

File system instructions

Images that include custom functionality will need to modify the file system. A Dockerfile defines three instructions that modify the file system: COPY, VOLUME, and ADD. The Dockerfile for the first implementation should be placed in a file named mailer-logging.df:

```
FROM dockerinaction/mailer-base:0.6

COPY ["./log-impl", "${APPROOT}"]

RUN chmod a+x ${APPROOT}/${APP} && \

chown example:example /var/log

USER example:example

VOLUME ["/var/log"]

CMD ["/var/log/mailer.log"]
```

In this Dockerfile you used the image generated from mailer-base as the starting point. The three new instructions are COPY, VOLUME, and CMD. The COPY instruction will copy files from the file system where the image is being built into the build container. The COPY instruction takes at least two arguments. The last argument is the destina-tion, and all other arguments are source files. This instruction has only one unexpected feature: any files copied will be copied with file ownership set to root. This is the case regardless of how the default user is set before the COPY instruction. It's better to delay any RUN instructions to change file ownership until all the files that you need to update have been copied into the image.

The COPY instruction will honor both shell style and exec style arguments, just like ENTRYPOINT and other instructions. But if any of the arguments contains whitespace, then you'll need to use the exec form.

TIP Using the exec (or string array) form wherever possible is the best prac-tice. At a minimum, a Dockerfile should be consistent and avoid mixing styles.

This will make your Dockerfiles more readable and ensure that instructions behave as you'd expect without detailed understanding of their nuances.

The second new instruction is VOLUME. This behaves exactly as you'd expect if you understand what the --volume flag does on a call to docker run or docker create. Each value in the string array argument will be created as a new volume definition in the resulting layer. Defining volumes at image build time is more limiting than at run-time. You have no way to specify a bind-mount volume or read-only volume at image build time. This instruction will only create the defined location in the file system and then add a volume definition to the image metadata.

The last instruction in this Dockerfile is CMD. CMD is closely related to ENTRYPOINT instruction. They both take either shell or exec forms and are both used to start a process within a container. But there are a few important differences.

The CMD command represents an argument list for the entrypoint. The default entrypoint for a container is /bin/sh. If no entrypoint is set for a container, then the val-ues are passed, because the command will be wrapped by the default entrypoint. But if the entrypoint is set and is declared using the exec form, then you use CMD to set default arguments. This base for this Dockerfile defines the ENTRYPOINT as the mailer com-mand. This Dockerfile injects an implementation of mailer.sh and defines a default argument. The argument used is the location that should be used for the log file.

Before building the image, you'll need to create the logging version of the mailer program. Create a directory at ./log-impl. Inside that directory create a file named mailer.sh and copy the following script into the file:

```
#!/bin/sh

printf "Logging Mailer has started.\n"

while true

do

MESSAGE=$(nc -l -p 33333)
```

```
printf "[Message]: %s\n" "$MESSAGE" > $1

sleep 1

done
```

The structural specifics of this script are unimportant. All you need to know is that this script will start a mailer daemon on port 33333 and write each message that it receives to the file specified in the first argument to the program. Use the following command to build the mailer-logging image from the directory containing mailer-logging.df:

```
docker build -t dockerinaction/mailer-logging -f mailer-logging.df .
```

The results of this image build should be anti-climactic. Go ahead and start up a named container from this new image:

```
docker run -d --name logging-mailer dockerinaction/mailer-logging
```

The logging mailer should now be built and running. Containers that link to this implementation will have their messages logged to /var/log/mailer.log. That's not very interesting or useful in a real-world situation, but it might be handy for testing.

An implementation that sends email would be better for operational monitoring.

The next implementation example uses the Simple Email Service provided by Amazon Web Services to send email. Get started with another Dockerfile. Name this file mailer-live.df:

```
FROM dockerinaction/mailer-base:0.6
```

```
ADD ["./live-impl", "${APPROOT}"]

RUN apt-get update && \

apt-get install -y curl python && \

curl "https://bootstrap.pypa.io/get-pip.py" -o "get-pip.py" && \

python get-pip.py && \

pip install awscli && \

rm get-pip.py && \

chmod a+x "${APPROOT}/${APP}"

RUN apt-get install -y netcat

USER example:example

CMD ["mailer@dockerinaction.com", "pager@dockerinaction.com"]
```

This Dockerfile includes one new instruction, ADD. The ADD instruction operates simi-larly to the COPY instruction with two important differences. The ADD instruction will

■ Fetch remote source files if a URL is specified

■ Extract the files of any source determined to be an archive file

The auto-extraction of archive files is the more useful of the two. Using the remote fetch feature of the ADD instruction isn't good practice. The reason is that although the feature is convenient, it provides no mechanism for cleaning up unused files and results in additional layers. Instead, you should use a chained RUN instruction like the third instruction of mailer-live.df.

The other instruction to note in this Dockerfile is the CMD instruction, where two arguments are passed. Here you're specifying the From and To fields on any emails that are sent. This differs from mailer-logging.df, which specifies only one argument.

Next, create a new subdirectory named live-impl under the location containing mailer-live.df. Add the following script to a file in that directory named mailer.sh:

```sh
#!/bin/sh

printf "Live Mailer has started.\n"

while true

do

MESSAGE=$(nc -l -p 33333)

aws ses send-email --from $1 \

--destination {\"ToAddresses\":[\"$2\"]} \

--message "{\"Subject\":{\"Data\":\"Mailer Alert\"},\
\"Body\":{\"Text\":{\"Data\":\"$MESSAGE}\"}}}"

sleep 1

done
```

The key takeaway from this script is that, like the other mailer implementation, it will wait for connections on port 33333, take action on any received messages, and then sleep for a moment before waiting for another message. This time, though, the script will send an email using the Simple Email Service command-line tool. Build and start a container with these two commands:

```
docker build -t dockerinaction/mailer-live -f mailer-live.df

docker run -d --name live-mailer dockerinaction/mailer-live
```

If you link a watcher to these, you'll find that the logging mailer works as advertised. But the live mailer seems to be having difficulty connecting to the Simple Email Service to send the message. With a bit of investigation, you'll eventually realize that the container is misconfigured. The aws program requires certain environment variables to be set.

You'll need to set AWS_ACCESS_KEY_ID, AWS_SECRET_ACCESS_KEY, and AWS_DEFAULT_REGION in order to get this example working. Discovering execution preconditions this way can be frustrating for users. Section 8.4.1 details an image design pattern that reduces this friction and helps adopters.

Before you get to design patterns, you need to learn about the final Dockerfile instruction. Remember, not all images contain applications. Some are built as platforms for downstream images. Those cases specifically benefit from the ability to inject downstream build-time behavior.

Injecting downstream build-time behavior

Only one Dockerfile instruction isn't covered in the primer. That instruction is ONBUILD. The ONBUILD instruction defines instructions to execute if the resulting image is used as a base for another build. For example, you could use ONBUILD instruc-tions to compile a program that's provided by a downstream layer. The upstream Dockerfile copies the contents of the build directory into a known location and then compiles the code at that location. The upstream Dockerfile would use a set of instructions like this:

ONBUILD COPY [".", "/var/myapp"]

ONBUILD RUN go build /var/myapp

The instructions following ONBUILD instructions aren't executed when their contain-ing Dockerfile is built. Instead, those instructions are recorded in the resulting image's metadata under ContainerConfig.OnBuild. The previous instructions would result in the following metadata inclusions:

...

"ContainerConfig": {

...

"OnBuild": [

"COPY [\".\", \"/var/myapp\"]",

"RUN go build /var/myapp"

],

...

This metadata is carried forward until the resulting image is used as the base for another Dockerfile build. When a downstream Dockerfile uses the upstream image (the one with the ONBUILD instructions) in a FROM instruction, those ONBUILD instruc-tions are executed after the FROM instruction and before the next instruction in a Dockerfile.

Consider the following example to see exactly when ONBUILD steps are injected into a build. You need to create two Dockerfiles and execute two build commands to get the full experience. First, create an upstream Dockerfile that defines the ONBUILD instructions. Name the file base.df and add the following instructions:

```
FROM busybox:latest

WORKDIR /app

RUN touch /app/base-evidence

ONBUILD RUN ls -al /app
```

You can see that the image resulting from building base.df will add an empty file named base-evidence to the /app directory. The ONBUILD instruction will list the con-tents of the /app directory at build time, so it's important that you not run the build in quiet mode if you want to see exactly when changes are made to the file system.

The next file to create is the downstream Dockerfile. When this is built, you will be able to see exactly when the changes are made to the resulting image. Name the file downstream.df and include the following contents:

```
FROM dockerinaction/ch8_onbuild
 RUN touch downstream-evidence

RUN ls -al .
```

This Dockerfile will use an image named dockerinaction/ch8_onbuild as a base, so that's the repository name you'll want to use when you build the base. Then you can see that the downstream build will create a second file and then list the contents of /app again.

With these two files in place, you're ready to start building. Run the following to create the upstream image:

```
docker build -t dockerinaction/ch8_onbuild -f base.df .
```

The output of the build should look like this:

```
Sending build context to Docker daemon 3.072 kB
```

```
Sending build context to Docker daemon
```

```
Step 0 : FROM busybox:latest
```

---> e72ac664f4f0

Step 1 : WORKDIR /app

---> Running in 4e9a3df4cf17

---> a552ff53eedc

Removing intermediate container 4e9a3df4cf17 Step 2 : RUN touch /app/base-evidence ---> Running in 352819bec296

---> bf38c3e396b2

Removing intermediate container 352819bec296 Step 3 : ONBUILD run ls -al /app ---> Running in fd70cef7e6ca

---> 6a53dbe28364

Removing intermediate container fd70cef7e6ca Successfully built 6a53dbe28364

Then build the downstream image with this command:

docker build -t dockerinaction/ch8_onbuild_down -f downstream.df .

The results clearly show when the ONBUILD instruction (from the base image) is executed:

Sending build context to Docker daemon 3.072 kB

Sending build context to Docker daemon

Step 0 : FROM dockerinaction/ch8_onbuild

Executing 1 build triggers Trigger 0, RUN ls -al /app Step 0 : RUN ls -al /app

---> Running in dd33ddea1fd4 total 8

drwxr-xr-x
2
root
root
4096
Apr 20
23:08 .

drwxr-xr-x
30
root
root
4096
Apr
20
23:08 ..

-rw-r--r--
1
root
root
0
Apr

23:08 base-evidence

---> 92782cc4e1f6

Removing intermediate container dd33ddea1fd4 Step 1 : RUN touch downstream-evidence ---> Running in 076b7e110b6a

---> 92cc1250b23c

Removing intermediate container 076b7e110b6a

Step 2 : RUN ls -al .

---> Running in b3fe2daac529

total 8

drwxr-xr-x

2

root

root

4096

Apr 20

23:08 .

drwxr-xr-x

31

root

root

4096

Apr 20

23:08 ..

-rw-r--r--

1

root

root

0

Apr 20

23:08 base-evidence

-rw-r--r--

1

root

```
root

0

Apr 20

23:08 downstream-evidence


---> 55202310df7b
```

Removing intermediate container b3fe2daac529 Successfully built 55202310df7b

You can see the builder registering the ONBUILD instruction with the container meta-data in step 3 of the base build. Later, the output of the downstream image build shows which triggers (ONBUILD instructions) it has inherited from the base image. The builder discovers and processes the trigger immediately after step 0, the FROM instruc-tion. The output then includes the result of the RUN instruction specified by the trigger. The output shows that only evidence of the base build is present. Later, when the builder moves on to instructions from the downstream Dockerfile, it lists the con-tents of the /app directory again. The evidence of both changes is listed.

That example is more illustrative than it is useful. You should consider browsing Docker Hub and looking for images tagged with onbuild suffixes to get an idea about how this is used in the wild. Here are a few of my favorites:

- https://registry.hub.docker.com/_/python/

- https://registry.hub.docker.com/_/golang/

- https://registry.hub.docker.com/_/node/

Whatever tooling you choose to use, you'll always need to consider a few image design aspects. You'll need to ask yourself whether the software running in your container requires any startup assistance, supervision, monitoring, or coordination with other in-container processes. If so, then you'll need to include a startup script or initialization program with the image and install it as the entrypoint.

Environmental preconditions validation

Failure modes are difficult to communicate and can catch someone off guard if they occur at arbitrary times. If container configuration problems always cause failures at startup time for an image, users can be confident that a started container will keep running.

In software design, failing fast and precondition validation are best practices. It makes sense that the same should hold true for image design. The preconditions that should be evaluated are assumptions about the context.

Docker containers have no control over the environment where they're created. They do, however, have control of their own execution. An image author can solidify the user experience of their image by introducing environment and dependency vali-dation prior to execution of the main task. A container user will be better informed about the requirements of an image if containers built from that image fail fast and display descriptive error messages.

For example, WordPress requires certain environment variables to be set or container links to be defined. Without that context, WordPress would be unable to connect to the database where the blog data is stored. It would make no sense to start WordPress in a container without access to the data it's supposed to serve. WordPress images use a script as the container entrypoint. That script validates that the container context is set in a way that's compatible with the contained version of WordPress. If any required condition is unmet (a link is undefined or a variable is unset), then the script will exit before starting WordPress, and the container will stop unexpectedly.

This type of startup script is generally use-case specific. If you're packaging a specific piece of software in an image, you'll need to write the script yourself. Your script should validate as much of the assumed context as possible. This should include the following:

- Presumed links (and aliases)

- Environment variables

- Network access

- Network port availability

- Root file system mount parameters (read-write or read-only)

- Volumes

- Current user

You can use whatever scripting or programming language you want to accomplish the task. In the spirit of building minimal images, it's a good idea to use a language or scripting tool that's already included with the image. Most base images ship with a shell like /bin/sh or /bin/bash. Shell scripts are the most common for that reason.

Consider the following shell script that might accompany a program that depends on a web server. At container startup, this script enforces that either another container has been linked to the web alias and has exposed port 80 or the WEB_HOST environment variable has been defined:

```
#!/bin/bash

set -e

if [ -n "$WEB_PORT_80_TCP" ]; then

if [ -z "$WEB_HOST" ]; then

WEB_HOST='web'

else

echo >&2 '[WARN]: Linked container, "web" overridden by $WEB_HOST.' echo >&2
"===> Connecting to WEB_HOST ($WEB_HOST)"

fi

fi

if [ -z "$WEB_HOST" ]; then

echo >&2 '[ERROR]: specify a linked container, "web" or WEB_HOST environ-

ment variable'

exit 1

fi

exec "$@" # run the default command
```

If you're unfamiliar with shell scripting, this is an appropriate time to learn it. The topic is approachable, and there are several excellent resources for self-directed learn-ing. This specific script uses a pattern where both an environment variable and a container link are tested. If the environment variable is set, the container link will be ignored. Finally, the default command is executed.

Images that use a startup script to validate configuration should fail fast if someone uses them incorrectly, but those same containers may fail later for other reasons. You can combine startup scripts with container restart policies to make reliable containers. But container restart policies are not perfect solutions. Containers that have failed and are waiting to be restarted aren't running. This means that an operator won't be able to execute another process within a container that's in the middle of a backoff window. The solution to this problem involves making sure the container never stops.

Initialization processes

UNIX-based computers usually start an initialization (init) process first. That init pro-cess is responsible for starting all the other system services, keeping them running, and shutting them down. It's often appropriate to use an init-style system to launch, manage, restart, and shut down container processes with a similar tool.

Init processes typically use a file or set of files to describe the ideal state of the ini-tialized system. These files describe what programs to start when to start them, and what actions to take when they stop. Using an init process is the best way to launch

multiple programs, clean up orphaned processes, monitor processes, and automati-cally restart any failed processes.

If you decide to adopt this pattern, you should use the init process as the entry-point of your application-oriented Docker container. Depending on the init program you use, you may need to prepare the environment beforehand with a startup script.

For example, the runit program doesn't pass environment variables to the pro-grams it launches. If your service uses a startup script to validate the environment, it won't have access to the environment variables it needs. The best way to fix that problem might be to use a startup script for the runit program. That script might write the environment variables to some file so the startup script for your application can access them.

There are several open source init programs. Full-featured Linux distributions ship with heavyweight and full-featured init systems like SysV, Upstart, and systemd. Linux Docker images like Ubuntu, Debian, and CentOS typically have their init programs installed but nonfunctioning out of the box. These can be complex to configure and typically have hard dependencies on resources that require root access. For that reason, the community has tended toward the use of lighter-weight init programs.

Popular options include runit, BusyBox init, Supervisord, and DAEMON Tools. These all attempt to solve similar problems, but each has its benefits and costs. Using an init process is a best practice for application containers, but there's no perfect init program for every use case. When evaluating any init program for use in a container, consider these factors:

- Additional dependencies the program will bring into the image

- File sizes

- How the program passes signals to its child processes (or if it does)

- Required user access

- Monitoring and restart functionality (backoff-on-restart features are a bonus)

- Zombie process cleanup features

Whichever init program you decide on, make sure your image uses it to boost adopter confidence in containers created from your image. If the container needs to fail fast to communicate a configuration problem, make sure the init program won't hide that failure.

These are the tools at your disposal to build images that result in durable contain-ers. Durability is not security, and although adopters of your durable images might trust that they will keep running as long as they can, they shouldn't trust your images until they've been hardened.

Building hardened application images

As an image author, it's difficult to anticipate all the scenarios where your work will be used. For that reason, harden the images you produce whenever possible. *Hardening an image* is the process of shaping it in a way that will reduce the attack surface inside any Docker containers based on it.

A general strategy for hardening an application image is to minimize the software included with it. Naturally, including fewer components reduces the number of potential vulnerabilities. Further, building minimal images keeps image download times short and helps adopters deploy and build containers more rapidly.

There are three things that you can do to harden an image beyond that general strategy. First, you can enforce that your images are built from a specific image. Second, you can make sure that regardless of how containers are built from your image, they will have a sensible default user. Last, you should eliminate a common path for root user escalation.

The image identifiers discussed so far in this book are all designed to allow an author to update images in a transparent way to adopters. An image author chooses what image their work will be built on top of, but that layer of transparency makes it diffi-cult to trust that the base hasn't changed since it was vetted for security problems. Since Docker 1.6, the image identifier has included an optional digest component.

An image ID that includes the digest component is called a content addressable image identifier (CAIID). This refers to a specific layer containing specific content, instead of simply referring to a particular and potentially changing layer.

Now image authors can enforce a build from a specific and unchanging starting point as long as that image is in a version 2 repository. Append an @ symbol followed by the digest in place of the standard tag position.

Use docker pull and observe the line labeled digest in the output to discover the digest of an image from a remote repository. Once you have the digest, you can use it as the identifier to FROM instructions in a Dockerfile. For example, consider the follow-ing, which uses a specific snapshot of debian:jessie as a base:

```
docker pull debian:jessie

# Output:

# ...

# Digest: sha256:d5e87cfcb730...

# Dockerfile:

FROM debian@sha256:d5e87cfcb730...

...
```

Regardless of when or how many times the Dockerfile is used to build an image, they will all use the content identified with that CAIID as their base. This is particularly use-ful for incorporating known updates to a base into your images and identifying the exact build of the software running on your computer.

Although this doesn't directly limit the attack surface of your images, using CAIIDs will prevent it from changing without your knowledge. The next two practices do address the attack surface of an image.

User permissions

The known container breakout tactics all rely on having system administrator privileges inside the container. This section covers standard practices for establishing reasonable user defaults for images.

First, please understand that a Docker user can always override image defaults when they create a container. For that reason, there's no way for an image to prevent containers from running as the root user. The best things an image author can do are create other non-root users and establish a non-root default user and group.

Dockerfile includes a USER instruction that sets the user and group in the same way you would with the docker run or docker create command. The instruction itself was covered in the Dockerfile primer. This section is about considerations and best practices.

The best practice and general guidance is to drop privileges as soon as possible. You can do this with the USER instruction before any containers are ever created or with a startup script that's run at container boot time. The challenge for an image author is to determine the earliest appropriate time.

If you drop privileges too early, the active user may not have permission to complete the instructions in a Dockerfile. For example, this Dockerfile won't build correctly:

```
FROM busybox:latest

USER 1000:1000

RUN touch /bin/busybox
```

Building that Dockerfile would result in step 2 failing with a message like touch: /bin/busybox: Permission denied. File access is obviously impacted by user changes. In this case UID 1000 doesn't have permission to change the ownership of the file /bin/busybox. That file is currently owned by root. Reversing the second and third lines would fix the build.

The second timing consideration is the permissions and capabilities needed at runtime. If the image starts a process that requires administrative access at runtime, then it would make no sense to drop user access to a non-root user before that point. For example, any process that needs access to the system port range (1–1024) will need to be started by a user with administrative (at the very least CAP_NET_ADMIN) privileges. Consider what happens when you try to bind to port 80 as a non-root user with Netcat. Place the following Dockerfile in a file named UserPermissionDenied.df:

```
FROM busybox:latest

USER 1000:1000

ENTRYPOINT ["nc"]

CMD ["-l", "-p", "80", "0.0.0.0"]
```

Build the Dockerfile and run the resulting image in a container. In this case the user (UID 1000) will lack the required privileges, and the command will fail:

```
docker
build \

-t
dockerinaction/ch8_perm_denied \

-f
UserPermissionDenied.df \

.


docker
run dockerinaction/ch8_perm_denied

# Output:

# nc: bind: Permission denied
```

In cases like these, you may see no benefit in changing the default user. Instead, any startup scripts that you build should take on the responsibility of dropping permissions as soon as possible. The last question is which user should be dropped into?

Docker currently lacks support for the Linux USR namespace. This means that UID 1000 in the container is UID 1000 on the host machine. All other aspects apart from the UID and GID are segregated, just as they would be between computers. For exam-ple, UID 1000 on your laptop might be your username, but the username associated with UID 1000 inside a BusyBox container is default.

Ultimately, until Docker adopts the USR namespace, it will be difficult for image authors to know which UID/GID is appropriate to use. The only thing we can be sure of is that it's inappropriate to use common or system-level UID/GIDs where doing so can be avoided. With that in mind, it's still burdensome to use raw UID/GID numbers. Doing so makes scripts and Dockerfiles less readable. For that reason, it's typical for image authors to include RUN instructions that create users and groups used by the image. The following is the second instruction in a Postgres Dockerfile:

add our user and group first to make sure their IDs get assigned

consistently, regardless of whatever dependencies get added

RUN groupadd -r postgres && useradd -r -g postgres postgres

This instruction simply creates a postgres user and group with automatically assigned UID and GID. The instruction is placed early in the Dockerfile so that it will always be cached between rebuilds, and the IDs remain consistent regardless of other users that are added as part of the build. This user and group could then be used in a USER instruction. That would make for a safer default. But Postgres containers require ele-vated privileges during startup. Instead, this particular image uses a su or sudo-like program called gosu to start the Postgres process as the postgres user. Doing so makes sure that the process runs without administrative access in the container.

User permissions are one of the more nuanced aspects of building Docker images. The general rule you should follow is that if the image you're building is designed to run some specific application code, then the default execution should drop user per-missions as soon as possible.

A properly functioning system should be reasonably secure with reasonable defaults in place. Remember, though, an application or arbitrary code is rarely perfect and could be intentionally malicious. For that reason, you should take additional steps to reduce the attack surface of your images.

SUID and SGID permissions

The last hardening action to cover is the mitigation of SUID or SGID permissions. The well-known file system permissions (read, write, execute) are only a portion of the set defined by Linux. In addition to those, two are of particular interest: SUID and SGID.

These two are similar in nature. An executable file with the SUID bit set will always execute as its owner. Consider a program like /usr/bin/passwd, which is owned by the root user and has the SUID permission set. If a non-root user like bob executes passwd, he will execute that program as the root user. You can see this in action by building an image from the following Dockerfile:

FROM ubuntu:latest

Set the SUID bit on whoami RUN chmod u+s /usr/bin/whoami
Create an example user and set it as the default

RUN adduser --system --no-create-home --disabled-password --disabled-login \ --shell /bin/sh example

USER example

Set the default to compare the container user and

the effective user for whoami

CMD printf "Container running as: %s\n" $(id -u -n) && \

printf "Effectively running whoami as: %s\n" $(whoami)

Once you've created the Dockerfile, you need to build an image and run the default command in a container:

docker build -t dockerinaction/ch8_whoami .

docker run dockerinaction/ch8_whoami

Doing so prints results like these to the terminal:

Container running as: example

Effectively running whoami as: root

The output of the default command shows that even though you've executed the whoami command as the example user, it's running from the context of the root user. The SGID works similarly. The difference is that the execution will be from the owning group's context, not the owning user.

Running a quick search on your base image will give you an idea of how many and which files have these permissions:

docker run --rm debian:wheezy find / -perm +6000 -type f

It will display a list like this:

/sbin/unix_chkpwd

/bin/ping6

/bin/su

/bin/ping

/bin/umount

/bin/mount

/usr/bin/chage

/usr/bin/passwd

/usr/bin/gpasswd

/usr/bin/chfn

/usr/bin/newgrp

/usr/bin/wall

/usr/bin/expiry

/usr/bin/chsh

/usr/lib/pt_chown

This command will find all of the SGID files:

docker run --rm debian:wheezy find / -perm +2000 -type f

The resulting list is much shorter:

/sbin/unix_chkpwd

/usr/bin/chage

/usr/bin/wall

/usr/bin/expiry

Each of the listed files in this particular image has the SUID or SGID permission, and a bug in any of them could be used to compromise the root account inside a container. The good news is that files that have either of these permissions set are typically useful during image builds but rarely required for application use cases. If your image is going to be running software that's arbitrary or externally sourced, it's a best practice to mitigate this risk of escalation.

Fix this problem and either delete all these files or unset their SUID and SGID permissions. Taking either action would reduce the image's attack surface. The following Dockerfile instruction will unset the SUID and GUID permissions on all files currently in the image:

RUN for i in $(find / -type f \(-perm +6000 -o -perm +2000 \)); \ do chmod ug-s $i; done

Hardening images will help users build hardened containers. Although it's true that no hardening measures will protect users from intentionally building weak containers, those measures will help the more unsuspecting and most common type of user.

Summary

Most Docker images are built automatically from Dockerfiles. This chapter covers the build automation provided by Docker and Dockerfile best practices. Before moving on, make sure that you've understood these key points:

- Docker provides an automated image builder that reads instructions from Dockerfiles.

- Each Dockerfile instruction results in the creation of a single image layer.

- Merge instructions whenever possible to minimize the size of images and layer count.

- Dockerfiles include instructions to set image metadata like the default user, exposed ports, default command, and entrypoint.

- Other Dockerfile instructions copy files from the local file system or remote location into the produced images.

- Downstream builds inherit build triggers that are set with ONBUILD instructions in an upstream Dockerfile.

- Startup scripts should be used to validate the execution context of a container before launching the primary application.

- A valid execution context should have appropriate environment variables set, network dependencies available, and an appropriate user configuration.

■ Init programs can be used to launch multiple processes, monitor those pro-cesses, reap orphaned child processes, and forward signals to child processes.

■ Images should be hardened by building from content addressable image identifiers, creating a non-root default user, and disabling or removing any executable with SUID or SGID permissions.

Conclusions

Both Docker Machine and Docker Swarm provide functionality that enhances the applications for the Docker Engine. These and other related technologies will help you apply what you have learned in this book as you grow from using Docker on a single computer into managing fleets of containers distributed across many computers. It is important to have a thorough understanding of these points as you grow into this space:

■ A user can use Docker Machine to create a local virtual machine or machine in the cloud with a single create command.

■ The Docker Machine env and config subcommands can be used to configure Docker clients to work with remote Docker Engines that were provisioned with Docker Machine.

■ Docker Swarm is a protocol that is backward-compatible with the Docker Remote API and provides clustering facilities over a set of member nodes.

■ A Swarm manager program implements the Swarm API and handles container scheduling for the cluster.

■ Docker Machine provides flags for provisioning both Swarm nodes and managers.

■ Docker Swarm provides three different scheduling algorithms that can be tuned through the use of filters.

■ Labels and other default attributes of a Docker Engine can be used as filtering criteria via container scheduling constraints.

■ Container scheduling affinities can be used to place containers on the same host as other containers or images that match a provided pattern or expression.

■ When any Docker client is configured to communicate with a Swarm endpoint, that client will interact with the entire Swarm as if it were a single Docker machine.

■ Docker Swarm will schedule dependent containers on the same node until multi-host networking is released or you provide another service-discovery mechanism and disable the dependency Swarm filter.

■ Multi-host networking will abstract container locality from the concerns of applications within Docker containers. Each container will be a host on the overlay network

www.ingramcontent.com/pod-product-compliance
Lightning Source LLC
LaVergne TN
LVHW051337050326
832903LV00031B/3591